# WHITETAIL
## Techniques & Tactics

CREATIVE
PUBLISHING
international

CHANHASSEN, MINNESOTA

www.creativepub.com

*President/CEO:* Michael Eleftheriou
*Vice President/Publisher:* Linda Ball
*Vice President/Retail Sales & Marketing:* Kevin Haas

WHITETAIL TECHNIQUES & TACTICS

*Executive Editor, Outdoor Group:* Don Oster
*Editorial Director:* David R. Maas
*Managing Editor:* Jill Anderson
*Senior Editor:* Steven Hauge
*Senior Creative Director:* Brad Springer
*Senior Art Director:* David W. Schelitzche
*Photo Editor:* Angela Hartwell
*Director, Production Services:* Kim Gerber
*Print Production Manager:* Helga Thielen
*Production Staff:* Stephanie Barakos, Laura Hokkanen
*Cover Photo:* Mark Kayser
*Contributing Photographers:* Charles J. Alsheimer, Scott Bestul, Denver Bryan, Amos Chan, Robert DiScalfani, Donald M. Jones, Mark Kayser, Bill Kinney, Lance Krueger, Bill Lea, Stephen W. Maas, Bill Marchel, Aaron Fraser Pass
*Contributing Illustrators:* William Bramhall, Gary Cooley, Gary Gretter

*Printed on American paper by:* Quebecor World
10  9  8  7  6  5  4  3  2

Library of Congress Cataloging-in-Publication Data

Whitetail techniques & tactics.
    p. cm. -- (Complete hunter)
  ISBN 0-86573-158-6
    1. White-tailed deer hunting.  I. Title: Whitetail techniques and tactics. II. Creative Publishing International. III. Complete hunter (Creative Publishing International)

SK301 . W463 2001
799.2'7652--dc21

2001017259

# CONTENTS

## ABOUT WHITETAILS

8    Deer Sign Language …*by Peter J. Fiduccia*

14   Whitetails & Acorns …*by Scott Bestul*

16   Secrets of the Rut …*by Peter J. Fiduccia*

22   How Whitetails Move …*by Dwight Schuh*

## HUNTING TECHNIQUES

28   Find Your Buck Now
      …*by Peter J. Fiduccia & Monte Burch*

32   Patterning Whitetails …*by Dwight Schuh*

34   Tips for Opening Day …*by Monte Burch*

38   The Magnificent Seven …*by Monte Burch*

42   The Still-Hunting Advantage …*by Jay Cassell*

46   Glass & Stalk …*by Don Oster*

50   Whitetail Tactics for Three Stages of the Rut
      …*by Peter J. Fiduccia*

54   Deer Tricks …*by Peter J. Fiduccia*

62   Decoying …*by Don Oster*

66   Talk to the Animals …*by Jay Cassell*

68   The Human Scent Factor …*by Dwight Schuh*

70   Late Season Is Drive Time …*by Jay Cassell*

72   Snow Bucks …*by Gerald Almy*

76   Deer Hunting's Terrible 10 …*by Gerald Almy*

## MAKING THE SHOT

82   The Point of Aim …*by Tom Gresham*

86   The Quest for Accuracy …*by Grits Gresham*

## EQUIPMENT

90   Easy-Shooting Rifles …*by Clair Rees*

94   How Scopes Help You Hit …*by Wayne van Zwoll*

98   Slug-Gunning for Deer
      …*by Philip Bourjaily & Mike Bleech*

101   The Troubled Shooter …*by Aaron Fraser Pass*

104   The Muzzleloading Revolution …*by Gerald Almy*

110   Handgunning for Deer …*by Tom Gresham*

112   Get That Bow Out of the Closet
      …*by Dwight Schuh*

114   Quick & Easy Stands …*by Dwight Schuh*

118   Building a Permanent Stand …*by Jay Cassell*

120   The Height of Foolishness …*by Tom McIntyre*

122   Recognize These Guys? …*by Peter J. Fiduccia*

124   Field-Dressing Whitetails
      …*by the Editors of Creative Publishing
       international*

126   About the Contributors

# INTRODUCTION

*Deer hunting means different things to different people.*
*To Spanish philosopher José Ortega y Gasset,*
*"by hunting man succeeds . . . in separating himself*
*from the present, and in renewing the primitive situation."*
*Man hunts to reconnect with nature.*

Theodore Roosevelt felt that "the finding and killing of the game is after all but a part of the whole." He extolled the virtues of hunting in rugged wilderness, and of adventuring into new territory. Hunting built character and manliness.

To most of us, hunting – and, in particular, deer hunting – is a way to break away from our daily lives and to get out into the woods, matching wits with an extremely wary quarry. Whether we succeed or fail in our hunt depends not so much on luck, but on our preparation, our skill. The hunter who gets a deer every year does his homework: He scouts his hunting territory before the season, patterning deer movements, mapping their travel routes, bedding and feeding areas; when afield, he hunts slowly and methodically, always alert, always ready; and if an opportunity arises, he meets the challenge, and dispatches his quarry as quickly and efficiently as possible.

It doesn't end there, either. In the offseason, the serious hunter studies. He watches hunting videos, he attends hunting seminars at sportsmen's shows, he reads magazines and books about hunting. For the good hunter, the learning process never stops. There are always more tactics to know, more advantages to gain, more deer habits to understand and analyze. And make no mistake, the whitetail deer is not stupid. It has adapted to man and his encroachment upon the wilderness. In fact, deer are absolutely thriving as we enter the 21th century. At this writing, there are an estimated 27 million whitetail deer in North America, many more than were here when white settlers first set foot upon the continent. Each year, almost 10 million people hunt them. Perhaps 20 percent are successful.

We have put together this book, *Whitetail Techniques & Tactics,* for the sole purpose of helping you, the whitetail deer hunter, improve your odds for success. We chose some of country's top big-buck hunters and asked them to write about what they know best – deer hunting.

The book itself is divided into four fact-filled sections. The first, "About Whitetails," contains articles devoted to the animal and its habits. Understanding how whitetails feed, interact, travel and behave during the rut gives the reader a good foundation from which to build his hunting strategies.

From there, the book moves right into the second, perhaps most important section, on "Hunting Techniques." Here you'll find all the hard-core information you'll need to become a successful hunter: how to still-hunt, hunt from a stand and put on deer drives; how to use decoys, calls and scents; how to hunt the various stages of the rut; how to hunt in rain, snow, hot and cold; on opening day and closing day. It's all laid out for you like a road map.

"Making the Shot," section three, is all about shooting your gun or bow. You can get close to the biggest buck in the world, but if you can't shoot straight, from a variety of angles, you might as well go home. Here you'll find valuable tips on where to aim, how to shoot steadily, and how to become more accurate.

The "Equipment" section takes up where the previous section leaves off, delving into how to select and properly use scopes, slug guns, rifles, muzzleloaders, bows, plus all the gear you need during the course of a season: ammunition, tree stands, buck and doe decoys, and more.

As a special bonus, at the end of the book you'll find a step-by-step guide on how to field-dress a deer properly, so the meat can be butchered without waste, and then turned into fine tablefare.

The articles contained in *Whitetail Techniques & Tactics* teach, entertain, and inform. And while we won't guarantee that this book will help you shoot a Boone & Crockett class buck this coming season, we will assert that if you follow the advice found between the covers of this book, you will become a better deer hunter. We guarantee that.

*– Jay Cassell*

# ABOUT WHITETAILS

Successful whitetail hunters have one thing in common: They understand their quarry. Being serious students of deer behavior, these hunters study whitetails and work year-round to prepare for each season. Reading whitetail sign, they scout, map and study all of the features in their hunting area that deer use as bedding areas, sanctuaries, food supplies, feeding locations and travel corridors. Based on knowledge of deer behavior and movement, the hunter will plan techniques to be used as the season progresses.

Rub lines, scrape areas and the dominant buck's core area will be clearly identified, with the knowledge that these places will be hot spots during the rut year after year. The best locations for blinds or tree stands are planned well in advance of the season. Trophy hunters understand growth rates and antler development. They know the specific quality of some deer headgear in the area, be it from the shed that was found in last winter's snow or the 8-pointer that was passed up last season.

The combination of whitetail understanding with application of sound techniques and some preparatory hard work are all components of a consistently successful deer hunting program. Luck does play a part in any endeavor, but it can't be trusted for year-after-year hunting success.

— *Don Oster*

*Fresh rub*

*By Peter J. Fiduccia*

*How to interpret and take advantage of the rubs, scrapes, droppings and tracks that whitetails leave behind.*

# Deer Sign Language

**H**unters can never learn enough about white-tailed deer. They're puzzling, mysterious animals. But all deer do have a vulnerability, and that's the sign they leave behind. And by leaving clues to their whereabouts — be they flagrant or inconspicuous — deer provide us with the ability to put a kink in their defenses.

Consistently successful deer hunters are capable of going beyond the norm in understanding "sign." These hunters can open their minds to notice the slightest bit of deer information — sign most hunters neither recognize nor understand completely.

When I started deer hunting 27 years ago, an Adirondack old-timer gave me advice I have never forgotten. He said, "Pete, to be a good deer hunter, remember this: Chasin' deer is just like locatin' big trout. A good fisherman knows how to read the water, and once he reads water well, he'll catch fish regularly."

That's the year I made up my mind to make my deer hunting more than just putting an occasional buck in the freezer. And over the years, paying meticulous attention to sign has improved my deer hunting success immensely. By learning how to rank sign in order of its significance, you'll be more successful, too.

Before learning how to read sign more efficiently, however, a hunter must become more confident in his ability to hunt deer. Confidence is one of the most important and most overlooked elements in deer hunting. If you lack confidence, you may fail to notice (or even dismiss) good sign simply because you're not positive what you're looking at. A classic example of this is the hunter who constantly changes his hunting location. The next stand is always "where the deer are." Usually, this hunter winds up with nothing more than a lot of exercise for the day — all because he lacked confidence in his ability to recognize and evaluate sign.

## Scrapes:

The most pertinent information about scrapes is that they are sexual calling cards of both bucks and does. Although there are some half-dozen types of scrapes, you'll need to pay attention to only a few. The first scrapes are made in early October, and I refer to these as pre-rut scrapes. These are made when the most mature does of the herd come into a brief estrous cycle, usually lasting less than 36 hours. Bucks who come across this early season, unexpected estrous scent respond by making numerous small scrapes throughout their territory. These scrapes, which are usually not refreshened, are the

least likely scrapes to produce buck sightings. For the most part, hunters shouldn't pay much attention to them. The same philosophy applies to scrapes made by does, which often do not produce well for hunters. Just use these scrapes to confirm that there are deer in the area.

The scrapes that provide the most sightings of bucks are the primary, secondary and gregarious scrapes. Secondary scrapes are the most prevalent of all scrapes and are usually two to three feet round. Bucks will make between 20 and 30 such scrapes throughout their home range during the rutting season. Because of the sheer numbers of secondary scrapes, you can rest assured they are within a few hundred yards of a buck's core area. A hunter positioned over secondary scrapes is almost certain to see bucks because most of these scrapes are made where bucks spend a majority of their time.

When the rutting season reaches its peak, the secondary scrapes diminish

## MAP THE SIGN

*It may be helpful to mark prominent sign findings on a topo or hand-drawn map. Rub and scrape areas will be used in subsequent years.*

*Buck making a scrape*

*Dragging hoof prints in snow indicate a large deer, possibly a buck.*

in number and the remaining ones are used more frequently. These remaining scrapes become wet, churned up, and are transformed into primary scrapes. These primary scrapes, which are usually twice the size of a secondary scrape because of increased pawing, will undergo the peak of activity this time of year. Don't spend a lot of time around secondary scrapes in the early season. But keep track of the scrape activity; when the secondary scrapes become primary scrapes, hunt them until the rutting period is over.

A gregarious scrape can be either a primary or a secondary scrape that is used by several bucks of the same age group. Usually they are found in the same areas as secondary scrapes. These gregarious scrapes are nothing more than overused secondary scrapes. Because they are used by submissive bucks rather than the most aggressive bucks, they receive a lot of attention. They can be identified by their irregular shapes and beat-up look. Hunters watching such scrapes will usually score more quickly than if they watch any other type of scrape.

All scrapes are made in a relatively straight line over several hundred yards. Scrapes, like rubs, show up in the same places year after year. By identifying the most active scrapes in an area, hunters can count on bucks making scrapes in the same spot the following year. Even when a buck is shot near a certain scrape, do not forsake that exact area next year. Bucks are like big trout. If you catch one out of a certain hole, within a few days another fish will have claimed the territory.

### Tracks:

Tracks provide evidence that deer are living and traveling in specific areas. The clues left by tracks can often lead to more confusion than information, however. For instance, finding a single deep track that shows the dew claws only means you have discovered the track of a heavy deer — buck or doe. Beyond that, and despite what many old-timers might say, most biologists agree that it

is impossible to definitely identify the sex of the deer from its tracks.

There are dependable indications left by tracks, however, which will help a hunter make a more educated determination as to the probable sex of the deer. For example, tracks that show the spreading of the toes on a hoof and do not appear to be pigeon-toed generally belong to a buck. If you are following tracks that meander throughout the woods, you can bet you are on the trail of a doe. Bucks walk with a purpose. Their tracks will often move from point A to point B while taking the path of least resistance. When a buck meets an obstacle, he will often walk around it (unlike a doe, which will often walk under it) and then resume his line of direction. In addition, when a buck urinates, he drips urine into his tracks. A doe squats and urinates in one place.

Of course, the most reliable indication of a buck track is actually seeing the buck standing in the tracks. A close second is seeing tracks with drag marks behind them. Bucks are built differently at the hips than does, and sway and rock slightly side-to-side when they walk. This gives a buck the tendency to drag his feet, especially in the snow (left). A buck will drag his hooves rather than daintily lift them as a doe will. A track accompanied by a drag mark will most likely belong to a buck. The deeper and longer the drag mark, the older and heavier the buck. To further confirm your findings, measure the size of the track. Generally, tracks that measure $4\frac{1}{2}$ to $5\frac{1}{2}$ inches long belong to $2\frac{1}{2}$-year-old bucks. You can bet that tracks larger than $5\frac{1}{2}$ inches long are from mature bucks ($3\frac{1}{2}$ to $6\frac{1}{2}$ years old).

### Holding Areas:

Holding areas can also supply useful information. Deer tend to mill about in these areas before continuing to their destination. I refer to these spots as "social areas." They are often located where there is low brush, foxtails and cattails, and are usually found between bedding and feeding areas. Deer that congregate here leave behind discernible sign. These areas always contain numerous droppings of all sizes and matted high grass where deer have temporarily lain down. There is an excess of heavy trails coming in and out of these spots. And almost every social area I have ever encountered is within 100 yards of both bedding and feeding areas.

Social areas are good places to ambush deer, especially in the evening. The best way to avoid confusing a holding or social area with a bedding area is to look for available food. Social areas do not provide much in the way of food. Most offer only browse. A few will have overgrown grasses such as timothy. It is simply a semiprotected area for deer to hole up in prior to feeding in the evening or bedding in the morning.

## Rubs:

One of the most evident forms of deer sign is the buck rub. Bucks rub their antlers from late August until they shed them, often as late as March. The rub phenomenon is 10 times greater in frequency, size and intensity within the buck's range from

*Buck rubbing*

October to December. Rubs found during this time indicate where the buck is traveling to seek out does. Fresh rubs found from January on indicate the location of a buck's core area — an ideal place to plan an opening day archery ambush.

Buck rubs will also show you a predictable pattern regarding where a deer is traveling, what time of day he's using that particular route, and what food source he's heading toward most frequently. Most important, rubs can betray a buck's bedding area. For instance, when a hunter locates a spot where a buck has rubbed as many as 18 or more trees within 50 yards, he has discovered the buck's core area — where a buck spends 90 percent of his time. Bucks will rise several times a day from their beds to change position. Often, as they stretch, they will walk a few feet, defecate, and rub brush or a sapling before lying down again. By paying attention to wind direction and locating the most heavily used trail into this area, a hunter can plan a successful ambush for this deer.

The buck rubs most hunters come across can also be used to determine the travel pattern of a mature whitetail buck throughout his entire home range. When you discover a rub, lie or kneel down with the rub in front of you. Slowly look left and right. You should discover other rubs on trees, saplings or brush in front of you. Usually, each additional rub will be about 30 to 50 yards ahead of the other. Also, by knowing whether you are heading to or from feeding or bedding areas and which direction the rub is facing, you can tell if he is using this route in the morning or evening.

There are some misconceptions about rubs, too. A seasoned hunter never allows himself to be fooled into believing that all large rubs are made by large-racked bucks. This just isn't so. I have videotaped many small bucks, spikes and forkhorns rubbing large saplings (6 to 10 inches around) totally bare of bark as high as four feet from the ground. If I hadn't seen the small buck making the rub, I could have easily been duped into thinking the rub was made by a buck with a larger rack. Generally, smaller-racked bucks rub larger trees than most hunters believe. Larger-racked bucks, however, seldom rub smaller trees because of the lack of resistance the tree offers them. Trophy-sized bucks spend much less time rubbing their antlers on trees than they do thrashing and tearing up thick, resistant brush. When you find a large bush with roots that have been dislodged and branches broken and strewn about, you have found an area where a trophy buck has displayed his aggressiveness to all subordinate deer to see and smell.

Rubs made on branched trees 16 to 20 inches wide showing bark stripped on both trunks have most likely been made by bucks with wide racks. Rubs with many deep gouges are usually made from burrs and kickers on the antlers of mature bucks. If the tree or sapling is dripping sap, the rub was made within 48 hours. The most exciting aspect of finding a rub is that you will know it was made by a buck in your hunting area. If there are fresh shavings hanging from the tree and on the ground, look around — he may be only 100 yards ahead of you, establishing another rub marker.

## Droppings:

Another good indication that deer regularly use an area is the number of fresh piles of droppings you find.

According to the Wisconsin Department of Natural Resources, deer defecate about 13 times during a 24-hour period. Therefore, if you are hunting an area with a high whitetail population, analyzing this sign becomes a little more difficult. Here are some hints to help you select the information you need. Adult buck droppings are clustered and are larger than adult doe droppings. A good rule of thumb to determine the approximate age of a buck is that a single pellet measuring about three-quarters inch is from a buck about 2½ to 3½ years old. Larger pellets up to 1⅜ inches long are usually from the truly trophy-sized animals. Mature buck droppings are thicker, longer and generally clumped together in a shapeless mass rather than in single pellets. Finding a few dozen such droppings in an area perhaps 50 yards around is an indication you have found a buck's core (or preferred) bedding area. Consequently, you can eliminate the smaller loose pellets usually found in piles of 10 to 50 droppings; these belong to fawns, yearlings and does.

All deer droppings will change in texture and consistency as the deer's food source changes. This information will help you determine whether deer are browsing or grazing, and where you should post accordingly. If a deer is feeding on grasses or fruit, the feces will usually be in a loose mass composed of soft pellets. If you find such sign, hunt along routes leading to alfalfa fields or apple orchards.

When a deer is browsing on drier vegetation, such as twigs, branch tips and acorns, its droppings will be less moist because of a loss of mucus. Consequently, the pellets do not stick together when expelled from the deer. They will be hard to the touch, longer and separated. If you find this type of sign, plan your ambush accordingly. Posting in an alfalfa field when most of the deer dung you are finding is loose, hard and long will most likely prove to be futile, as the deer's droppings suggest they are not grazing but browsing.

When inspecting deer excrement, remember that weather affects its look and texture. If the pile you are examining is on top of a ridge, for instance, and is subject to wind and harsh sunlight and receives no moisture, it will dry much more quickly and appear to be stale, when in fact it may be fresher than you think. In places where deer pellets receive shade and moisture and are not exposed to wind, the opposite holds true.

You can eliminate the guesswork by picking up a few pellets and squeezing them between your thumb and index finger. Remember that pellets dry from the outside in. So one that looks fresh on the outside but is hard and dry and begins to break apart when squeezed is at least four days old. Shiny, fresh-looking pellets having the consistency of Play-Doh when squeezed may be very fresh.

You will often discover the freshest sign in and around bedding areas. When you locate an area with eight to 10 beds grouped within a short distance of one another, you have found the bedding area of does and fawns. But it

## WHITETAIL FACTS

## START EARLY

*The best time to scout and map out an area is during the spring before foliage develops. Rubs, scrapes, trails and bedding areas are highly visible and the intrusion will be long forgotten by next fall's season.*

*Study trails carefully to determine where the travel corridor leads and which sex is the primary user. Buck trails are more direct from point to point, doe trails meander through an area. At times, depending on terrain, a buck's trail will be faint and will parallel a heavily used doe trail.*

pays to investigate such an area. You can determine if a buck is within the group by measuring the size of the beds. Beds measuring about 2½ to 3 feet long are those of does, yearlings and fawns. However, beds measuring about 3½ to 4½ feet long are most likely those of a mature buck.

## Putting It All Together:

When you are out and looking for deer sign, remember to take a small tape measure with you. Doing so will eliminate guesswork, letting you accurately measure the size of droppings, the height and width of rubs, the size of beds and, later, the inside spread of your buck's rack! They're a useful tool for the hunter who reads sign.

The wise hunter doesn't stop reading sign after his buck is down. Now it's time to dissect and examine the digested and undigested contents of the four compartments of a deer's stomach. The information will let you know where and when the deer was feeding and what it was eating. The least-digested food is what the deer ate last. The food that's been further digested will be mushier, less identifiable, and will have to be investigated more closely — this is what the deer was feeding on first. By knowing the time of day your deer was killed, you will be able to backtrack through the stomach contents to discover the route the deer traveled. This information can be shared with hunting companions who haven't filled their tags. Or it can be used next season if the same general weather conditions and food patterns exist.

Deer sign allows a hunter to eliminate a majority of the guesswork and to place himself at the right place at the right time. Luck now takes a backseat to knowledge and skill. So, by taking the advice of that old Adirondack guide and learning to correctly "read the water," you too can become a better deer hunter.

## EARLY SEASON PATTERN

*By scouting tracks and trails (below), you find the buck is bedding in thick brush near the lake. His trail leads through a funnel to a crop field. Ambush him from treestands (x's) as he travels through the funnel.*

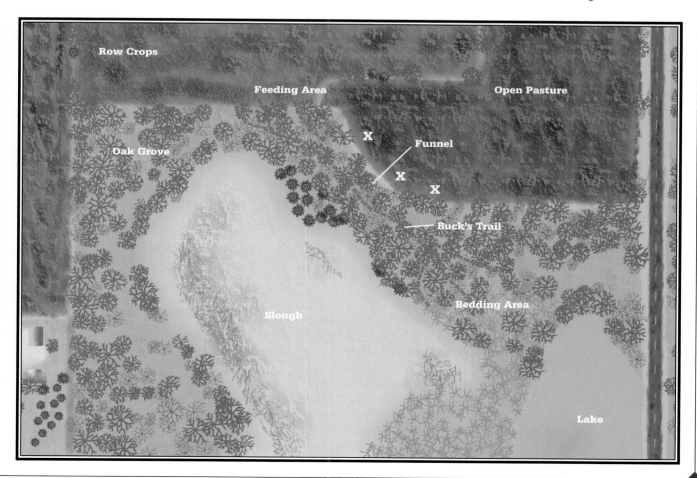

Row Crops

Feeding Area

Open Pasture

Oak Grove

X

Funnel

X

X

Buck's Trail

Slough

Bedding Area

Lake

# Whitetails & Acorns

*By Scott Bestul*

*Haven't seen many deer this season? Take a look beneath the oak stands.*

It happens occasionally: The deer that feed in those alfalfa fields, showing up like clockwork every evening, just stop showing up. Maybe the well-defined trails leading to that big patch of soybeans begin to show signs of disuse.

But the deer didn't just disappear. They've probably switched food sources — to an acorn-dropping oak back in the woods.

Whitetails eat a variety of foods, and agricultural crops are among their favorites. But when acorns are available, all bets are off. Available throughout whitetail range, acorns sustain deer (as well as grouse, bears, turkeys and squirrels) when succulent vegetation disappears each fall. In some areas, acorns comprise over half the whitetail's diet for a six-month period. They're a convenient source of the fat and protein that deer need for winter survival. Acorns are tasty (to deer) too — biologists note that once deer find an acorn-producing oak, they'll revisit it until most of the nuts are consumed. If that fruitful tree has some neighbors, it could be awhile before whitetails get serious about finding other food sources.

Individual oak species are typically divided into two families: white oak and red oak. You can identify a tree's family by its leaves. Red oak leaves end in sharp, spiny points, while white oaks show soft, rounded lobes. White oak acorns usually mature in one season; you can count on modest-but-consistent crops annually. Red oak acorns require two years to develop and are much more cyclical, varying from bumper crops (every three to five years) to near-zeros.

What causes such fluctuation in acorn numbers? Foresters muse over that one as some biologists ponder grouse cycles. Undoubtedly a number of variables determine nut production for an oak tree: site, soil, sunlight, rainfall, drought (a drought-stressed tree may produce a final bumper crop before

14

succumbing), with no one factor consistently predominating. To nail down specifics about acorn production in your hunting area, it's a good idea to talk to a local forester. Or go out and look for yourself.

If you hunt woodland that hosts both oak families – most of us do – you'll undoubtedly wonder which one deer prefer. The answer is dependent on many factors, not the least being the mood of the individual deer at the time. Biologists and foresters I've spoken with agree that white oak acorns contain less tannin than do red oak acorns. Therefore, whites are less bitter (or "more palatable," as one game manager put it). Also, since white oaks produce a crop virtually every year, deer may rely more on those acorns. Here all speculation ends. The party line is that deer love them all. Again, if you want to know what kind they're eating, scouting is the only sure way to find out.

Obviously you'll be a big step ahead if you can evaluate the acorn crop before hunting seasons begin. A mild, wet spring without a killing frost will get acorns off to a good start. Adequate summer rainfall helps, too. As fall approaches, visit mature oak stands (where trees are 30 feet tall and over) and scan the branches for acorns, using binoculars to search the loftiest crowns. If you spot an abundant acorn supply, note the location, either mentally or on a map. It's a solid bet that deer will be visiting these spots as acorns fall. The more areas like this you can locate, the greater your options will be once deer switch over to mast feeding.

With hunting seasons near, keep watching for signs that acorns are falling. An abundance of squirrels might tip you off to an acorn-laden autumn, but it could also mean that last fall's crop was the dandy. Gaggles of grays and flocks of fox squirrels could also mean that other nut crops – hickories, butternuts, etc. – are doing well. Determining each year's acorn crop, assuming you haven't been able to scout it, boils down to a quick visit to your favorite oak stands.

When acorns start dropping, you'll have plenty of evidence that deer have found them: Whitetails will churn up or scrape away leaf litter as they forage for the nuts. It'll be tempting to place a stand right in the thick of the sign, but it's better to set up on the trails deer use to enter the area. Deer probably won't be as alert while approaching, and they won't associate the feeding area with danger should you spook them. If you're lucky enough to find several acorn areas, spread out your hunting efforts – avoiding repeat vigils in one spot will keep it "fresh."

Hunting acorn-bearing oak stands may also be your best bet for taking a large buck. A trophy bowhunter from my region focuses almost exclusively on oak stands when hunting mature whitetails. Mike finds that bucks feed through these acorn-laden areas well into the morning as they head for bedding cover, and evening hunts have produced big bucks too shy to enter fields before dark. Even if you're just after venison, a good acorn crop is a true gold mine – one October evening last fall I watched 14 does gather under a single red oak. Now that's a true deer magnet.

## PATTERN THE DOES

*Finding the acorn woods where does feed regularly is your key to that big buck. Pattern the does and the dominant buck will be close by, checking out the does when the rut period begins.*

*Hunt acorn concentrations, and you may find big bucks like these.*

# Secrets of the Rut

*By Peter J. Fiduccia*

*Deer go through three distinct phases of breeding activity every fall; here's how to effectively hunt each one.*

I could see the antlers on the big buck glisten as he scurried back and forth in the small woodlot. It was noon and this was the third time I had seen the buck since I started hunting at 10:00 A.M. This time, it looked as if he would pass close enough to my stand for a shot.

As I watched, he suddenly stopped, whirled around, and began making a scrape. He frantically pawed out a large spot in the leaves, then began to urinate in it. A sound from a nearby cedar patch caught his attention. Moments later, a doe emerged from the cedars. The buck instantly chased after her; before I knew it the two had disappeared from sight.

*Common buck behavior during the pre-rut period includes making rubs and scrapes and nonaggressively sparring with other bucks. These sparring matches are more pushing and shoving than fighting and usually occur between a large buck and a smaller one.*

16

Ten minutes passed. Then, as I strained to listen, I could hear deer running in my direction. I had to listen hard because I couldn't see them with the hot noon sun glaring in my eyes. I made a soft adult doe grunt and here, running through the woods, came the same buck, searching for the impostor doe. He was beneath my tree stand in a flash, still searching when my arrow pierced through both his lungs. It was 12:30 P.M. on October 5th. I had been in the woods a total of 2½ hours, and in that time had seen three big bucks. The one I shot eventually scored high enough (135⅜) to make Pope & Young. All this because I was hunting the frenzy period of the pre-rut.

Recently, biologists have learned that whitetails begin mating as early as September and continue to breed through February. However, when applying this information to your hunting tactics, keep in mind there are exceptions to every rule.

Biologists refer to the three main phases of the rut as the pre-rut, the primary rut and the post-rut. Whitetails exhibit characteristic and behavioral changes during each phase, and hunters who know what to expect will have a decided edge when it comes to getting within range of a good-sized buck.

The biggest fallacy about the rut is that it's short and occurs only during cold weather. Cold weather does play a role in the activity levels of deer. However, it is not the genesis of the rut, as many hunters believe. During the rut, cold weather motivates bucks to move throughout the day seeking does. In extremely cold conditions, movement keeps them warmer. During a warm rutting period, on the other hand, deer become lethargic and bed throughout the day. They breed mostly at night when the air is considerably cooler.

This also holds true for sign such as rubs and scrapes. A warm rut means less sign, a cold rut means more sign, simply because there's much more movement during the colder weather. Warm fall or cold fall, however, all three phases of the rut will take place

## RUBBING

generally at the same time each year. Deer hunters can count on it.

## Stage 1: The Pre-Rut:

The most overlooked stage, and the one least capitalized on by hunters, is the pre-rut stage. Also called "the false rut," this typically occurs in early October. Archers who hunt during this time will attest to observing a yearly phenomenon regarding the rut where, all of a sudden, within a 24-hour period they begin to find a multitude of fresh scrapes throughout their hunting territory. What happens to cause this obviously intense breeding change in bucks? The onset of the pre-rut.

Because there is a lack of does in estrus in early September, bachelor herds of bucks continue with their normal behavior until early October, when a brief estrous cycle (18 to 36 hours) occurs. This brief cycle is brought on by the mature whitetail does (4½- to 5½-year-olds) that are coming into their first estrous period for the year. Once bucks discover the estrous pheromone permeating their range, their natural reaction is to start making scrapes and rubs. They'll continue to do this for up to 36 hours, all the while dashing throughout the woods in search of does.

*Bucks begin rubbing their antlers on trees, brush and shrubs as soon as the velvet starts to peel in September (above). Although the true function of rubbing is not totally understood, rubs are a form of communication and signify the presence of a dominant buck in the area. A buck may make as many as 30 to 40 rubs in one morning and up to 300 during a breeding season.*

*M*ature bucks sometimes engage in outright combat to establish dominance and breeding rights. These fights may last as long as 30 minutes. The most common wounds from these fights are inflicted on the neck. Combat results in a winner, with the loser quickly vacating the area under the threat of a final antler jab in his rear.

## RUT TIMING

*An avid hunter living in the suburbs of a large city claims he can time the rut peak by a sudden dramatic increase in rush hour car-deer accidents reported on morning drive-time radio.*

### Tactics:

If you learn to recognize the new scrape and deer activity signs as part of the "false" or pre-rut period, you will dramatically increase your chances of shooting a buck. By setting up around areas where bucks have opened new scrapes, for example, you can simply wait out your quarry, figuring that sooner or later a buck will come to check out his scrapes in hopes of finding a mature doe in estrus. Or you might try attracting a passing buck with a deer call or by rattling antlers. Another good tactic during this period is to make a mock scrape and agitate a buck into responding. All of these tactics will work during the pre-rut as bucks are eager to respond to the first signals of the start of the breeding season.

It is important to keep in mind that the pre-rut does not last long. Generally, throughout the East, the pre-rut occurs about the 7th through the 10th of October, give or take a couple of days either way.

Since only a few bucks actually get to mate during the pre-rut, the rest of the bucks become quite frustrated. This frustration is nature's way of laying the groundwork of behavior and activity that precedes the primary rut.

Every doe experiences an estrous cycle every 28 days until she is successfully bred. Therefore, a hunter can count 28 days forward from when he first discovers the above-mentioned activity during the pre-rut and he will place himself squarely within the primary rut.

### Stage 2: The Primary Rut:

The primary rut begins about the last week of October and lasts until about the last week of November. Think of this as a graph, with the time frames I mentioned above with peaks and valleys. However, jot down the peak period of the primary rut throughout the East, regardless of warm weather; it will inevitably fall sometime between November 8 and 17 – again, give or take a few days on either end.

## OVERHEAD BRANCH

*T*here will not be an active scrape without the presence of an overhead branch. The buck will rub his forehead on the branch, leaving scent on it. He may also smell and lick the branch, then freshen the scrape. Females visiting the scrape may also smell and lick the overhead branch.

There are several obvious signs after pre-rut that indicate the start of the primary rut. Bucks are seldom seen traveling together now. They have an ever-increasing intolerance for one another and will often engage in immediate aggressive behavior upon simply encountering other bucks. In addition, because of the building tension and continuing decrease in daylight, they will take out their anxieties more often on saplings or trees. Venting their frustrations also helps get them physically prepared for the inevitable battles that will come over the next few weeks. Once again, this buildup also accounts for a sharp increase in buck activity.

Unlike the pre-rut, when only a few mature does come into estrus, the primary rut has a majority of the does coming into their estrous cycle. This accounts for a dramatic increase in doe activity, too. Hunters will see does checking out buck scrapes, making scrapes of their own, running erratically through the woods, and avoiding fawns. Like female dogs, as they come closer to actually accepting males, they will begin to flag their tails. For deer, this simply means they will be seen carrying their tails in a horizontal position, off to one side. Hunters who take advantage of all of the above signs will find themselves at the right place at the right time. Because the primary rut falls during the time period when deer hunting pressure is heavy, I often use some unorthodox tactics to score on deer.

## Tactics:

During the primary rut, try hunting off-hours from 10:00 A.M. to 2:00 P.M.

*A buck's presence and readiness to breed are signified by scrapes (above). Regularly visited active or "hot" scrapes will convey a great deal of scent from the buck's rub-urination ritual. The combination of urine and tarsal smells is extremely strong. During the peak of the rut, hot scrapes become a focal point of breeding activity. These scrape spots tend to be reopened year after year.*

*The raised tail of the doe signals that she has entered estrus and will be willing to breed (above).*

*Because of the short general gun seasons in most states, the only hunters who can legally be afield during all stages of the rut are bowhunters and some muzzleloader hunters.*

This tactic works for a combination of reasons. First, you'll be hunting at a time of day when fewer hunters are in the woods. In addition, because deer are less pressured at this time, they move about more freely, giving you the chance to see more of them. Another tactic you might consider is to try using a variety of soft grunts (both buck and doe) throughout the day. Grunting works well throughout the entire primary rut period and should not be overlooked. Using certain agitating scents, such as buck urine and tarsal placed downwind from your stand, will also create opportunities that cannot be created in the pre- or post-rut periods, when deer are reacting to different stimuli.

## Stage 3: The Late or Post-Rut:

Count 28 days from the primary rut date, and you will have the prime time of the "late rut." During the late rut,

most of the immature (or latest born) does, and any other doe that has yet to be successfully bred, will come into estrus. I have had many hunters tell me that they have had success with rattling during the late rut, and this doesn't surprise me. Rattling can be effective into January and even February, as some does are still experiencing estrous cycles during these months.

The post-rut usually begins after a distinct low period in the primary rut. Throughout the East, the start of the post-rut usually begins around mid-December and runs for about 28 days. It is a period that is overlooked by many hunters who are sure that the rut is long over.

One sign to look for during this phase is a quick and dramatic increase in deer activity. Does that come into estrus during this period seem to have an intensity about finding bucks. They will often be seen trotting along depositing estrous urine. They will frequently make soft grunts, too. Any bucks scenting the estrous pheromone will quickly swarm to these estrous does. Often during the post-rut, hunters will see several bucks chasing one doe. It's almost as if the bucks have come to realize it's a "last chance" scenario.

## Tactics:

One tactic that works amazingly well during the post-rut is the use of sexual scents to attract bucks. In fact, estrous scents seem to work better now than they did during the primary rut, especially when applied from a drip dispenser attached to your boot. By wearing a dispenser, you can walk around your hunting location and create mock estrous trails of does. Such trails can attract bucks that might not have come near otherwise. Another post-rut strategy is to imitate the blat of a doe in heat. This deer call often brings bucks in on the run.

By recognizing that the rut is three to four months long, you can prevent yourself from falling into the habit of believing that your only chance for a big buck is during cold weather in November. Understand that there are three peak periods of rutting behavior from October through January, and plan your hunting accordingly. You'll see the difference.

*Once a buck finds an estrous doe, he may "tend" or follow her for several days until she is bred (below). During this time, the buck will feed very little. Some believe this is a stamina test for the buck, insuring that the healthiest bucks do most of the breeding.*

**TENDING**

# How *Whitetails Move*

*By Dwight Schuh*

*Now it's hunting season, and the deer you thought you knew by name have suddenly disappeared. Their whereabouts may surprise you.*

I've probably heard a thousand explanations for the disappearance of bucks at the beginning of hunting season: They got killed, they've become nocturnal, they've patterned the hunters. But I think in some cases, the disappearance – or better yet, the reappearance – of deer relates more to home range usage and natural movements than to any particular brainpower on the deer's part. Or to put it another way, you don't always have to outsmart them; you simply have to be in the right place at the right time.

## Travelers:

In fragmented habitat and areas with low deer numbers, whitetails, particularly bucks, roam much larger home ranges. In the hardwood forests of Mississippi, Dr. Harry Jacobson calculated the average annual ranges of does at 1820 acres and bucks at 3733 acres, with the largest at nearly 5500 acres. Whitetail researcher Dr. James Kroll said that bucks in Alberta may occupy core areas of 3000 acres or more and travel circuits of 20 to 25 miles during the rut, and that in the boreal forests of eastern Canada, bucks commonly travel 15 to 20 miles every five to seven days, searching for does. In the Dakotas and other prairie states with scattered cover, bucks may travel a dozen or more miles from one cover pocket to another. So they're here today, gone tomorrow.

### TRANSIENTS

Transient deer tend to be yearlings forced by their mothers from established home ranges to make room for new fawns. Many of them do not survive.

### HIDERS

By the advent of hunting season, most adult deer have become sedentary and virtually refuse to venture from familiar home ranges.

### MIGRATORS

In regions where whitetails migrate between summer and winter ranges, such as Idaho's Clearwater River drainage, search for "moving parties" — deer grouped at staging areas along the migration paths. To hunt these deer, you must be flexible.

### TRAVELERS

In fragmented habitat and areas with low deer numbers, whitetail bucks will travel circuits of anywhere from 15 to 25 miles, searching for does.

These long-distance travels explain why bucks in some areas disappear and suddenly reappear, especially during the rut. Under these conditions, a hunter's concern isn't so much being patterned by the deer, but getting in the path of a buck when he decides to show up. For far-ranging bucks, it often makes sense to analyze the country for the best travel routes, and then to stick with one good spot for several days until one of those roving bucks comes by.

### Shifters:

During a three-year study conducted in the early 90s on DeSoto National Wildlife Refuge in Nebraska, Kurt VerCauteren verified what most hunters know, that whitetails respond to hunting pressure. Near the DeSoto National Wildlife Refuge, where the Missouri River separates Iowa and Nebraska, VerCauteren witnessed that when the season opened in Nebraska, some deer swam to Iowa; when it opened in Iowa, they swam to Nebraska. (Even this proved hazardous, as one was hit and killed by a boat.)

Those that stayed at home also made distinct shifts. During the muzzleloader season on the DeSoto Refuge, eight collared deer moved into a strip of posted land 60x100 yards and remained there until the season closed.

Once the pressure let up, the deer quickly returned to their home ranges. In only two cases did deer stay in new ranges; most returned within two weeks.

The lesson? If bucks vanish in the face of heavy pressure, look for places where they might seek temporary refuge. Keep in mind that once the pressure eases, they'll probably return to their original home ranges. Plan to meet them there.

### Migrators:

In some regions, whitetails migrate between summer and winter ranges. Even in prairie and farm states, some whitetails migrate, but migrations are far more dramatic in the West, where deer travel from high summer ranges to low-elevation winter ranges.

In 1990 and 1991, Thomas Baumeister, as part of a continuing study, radio-collared 69 whitetails (26 adult bucks) in Idaho's Clearwater River drainage. He found that these deer occupied small summer home ranges of about 190 acres in the drainage's upper reaches. Then, in October and November, the deer migrated an average of 24 miles to winter ranges, some stopping at transition points along the way, others migrating straight through in four days. Many hunters believe deep snow triggers this migration, but so many deer migrated before any snow accumulation that weather can't be the only factor.

### Hiders:

In his Nebraska study, VerCauteren radio-collared several dozen deer and through telemetry relocated those deer a total of 17,000 times, plotting each one's home range. These ranges averaged 400 acres, although they varied greatly in size.

VerCauteren found that the most transient deer tended to be yearlings forced by their mothers from established home ranges to make room for new fawns. On average, transients dispersed 12 to 15 miles, although some subadults did travel 40 to 50 miles.

Many did not survive. "As soon as these deer leave familiar ground to fill vacant habitat off the refuge, they're vulnerable," VerCauteren said. "Of all the transients we

*Buck and doe home ranges vary in size throughout the year. Data from 20 years of radio-tracking in Texas show that adult bucks during the fall have the largest home ranges. This is the result of mature bucks traveling through several doe home ranges searching for a doe in estrus.*

|  | Spring | Summer | Fall | Winter |
|---|---|---|---|---|
| Buck Fawns | 310 | 160 | 140 | 150 |
| Yearling Bucks | 450 | 410 | 675 | 310 |
| Adult Bucks | 410 | 350 | 1090 | 290 |
| Doe Fawns | 390 | 160 | 110 | 275 |
| Yearling Does | 210 | 105 | 260 | 300 |
| Adult Does | 190 | 145 | 275 | 400 |

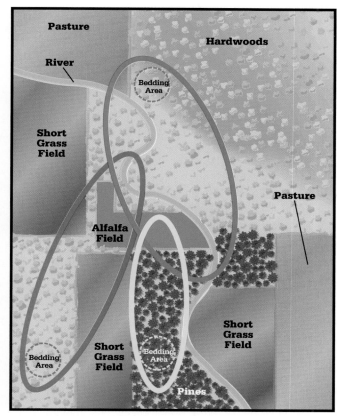

Farmland deer typically have small home ranges (colored ovals) because cover, food and water are close together.

brought him through a check station two years later. The hunter had shot the deer 200 yards from the original trapping location. VerCauteren surmises the buck had been living right there the whole time.

Hunters assume yearlings are easy prey because they're young and dumb, which is partly true, but the fact that they are forced into unfamiliar, marginal habitat is often what dooms them. Conversely, old deer become almost invisible not by smarts, but because they claim prime ranges where a sedentary life ensures a certain invincibility.

Obviously, transient yearlings can be easy pickings. But older, sedentary bucks are tough because they're on intimate ground and instantly recognize intrusion. To prevent detection, a hunter must stay out of their core areas; move constantly, hunting different locations each day to keep the deer guessing; and hunt only those spots where conditions, particularly wind, are perfect at that moment.

monitored, 16 percent were killed by vehicles and 36 percent by hunters." One year VerCauteren radio-collared five yearling bucks, and four left the refuge in August and September. The radio batteries went dead on two, so their fate is unknown, but the other three were killed by bowhunters that fall. Another buck summered securely in a small area, but then, in late October, swam the Missouri River and three days later was shot by a bowhunter.

In contrast, most adult deer became sedentary and virtually refused to venture from familiar home ranges; they had little reason to because food, water, security (and does during the rut) lay close at hand. One doe, for example, despite all intrusions, would not vacate a 40-acre parcel. And an old buck apparently had a similar lifestyle. On January 27, 1991, VerCauteren trapped and ear-tagged the buck and one month later caught him again in the same trap. Then VerCauteren never saw that deer again until a hunter

# NIGHT GHOSTS

*Some mature whitetail bucks go nocturnal from either hunting pressure or increased human presence in their territory.*

# HUNTING TECHNIQUES

**I**n accepting the challenge, deer hunters invade the whitetail's world, matching themselves against a quarry with clearly superior senses and survival instincts. Whitetails have the edge in spite of the hunter's high-tech equipment, enlightened knowledge and ability to reason. Hunters must scout, plan and make preparations to gain an edge. Their technique selection must allow for the range of weapon, differences in terrain, time of year, food availability, wind and daily weather conditions.

Glassing and stalking may be the best approach in open country or terrain too rough to walk. In heavy brush or deep woods, patterning deer movement and waiting in a tree stand along a trail may work best. Still-hunting or putting on the sneak is preferred by many hunters; gathering a small crowd and conducting a drive is preferred by others. Some hunters use calls to bring deer close with deer talk, while others use rattling horns and a decoy to pick a fight with a rut-crazed buck.

Beware of the acute senses of deer. Limit noise; deer hear and interpret unusual sounds as threats. Move slowly or not at all; deer instantly see movement but may not readily associate an inanimate shape with danger. Select field dress to blend with a tree, leaves, a brush pile, weeds, cornstalks or combinations of any of the above. To fool the whitetail's nose, some hunters practice rituals bordering on the fanatic or wear foul-smelling potions.

Despite our best efforts, the deer win consistently. Our failures only heighten the elation we feel when the wind is right and the techniques work as they do in all the outdoor stories.

*— Don Oster*

# Find *Your* Buck *Now*

*By Peter J. Fiduccia & Monte Burch*

*You know he's out there. Get him with old-time woods smarts and new technology.*

**H**ave you ever wondered how some hunters take deer year after year, even in heavily pressured areas where deer seem to disappear after opening day?

These hunters aren't lucky. They're good. And the reason they're good is that they scout their hunting territory year-round. They know the deer in their area — to the point where they can recognize individual bucks and even does — and they know where those deer go to feed, bed and escape from danger. While you're sitting at home, these hunters are out in the woods scouting.

The object of scouting is to locate a good buck (or bucks), then learn his feeding, travel and bedding routines long before the season starts. If you can, learn his escape routes as well; knowing where he goes when he's on the run will be of great value come hunting season.

Figuring out habit patterns isn't that difficult, as bucks tend to group together during summer. You can also

*Bachelor group*

determine which animals will have decent racks in the fall, because by July the main beams on most racks have started to turn forward. With binoculars, you can study a buck's growing rack and tell whether it's going to be large.

No matter where you hunt, you can count on the fact that a whitetail's movement patterns will be determined by five critical factors: food, water, cover, terrain and hunting pressure.

## Food & Water:

Being creatures of habit, deer generally stay on the same few hundred acres of land for their entire lives. Even when food sources change with the seasons, they usually won't move out of their home range in search of other things to eat.

If you hunt woodlots, locate oak trees yielding mast, wild apple trees, maples and other preferred food sources during preseason scouting trips. Finding oak trees that produce more acorns than other oaks in the immediate area, for example, will give you a hot spot to hunt while other hunters are still searching for deer.

On terrain other than woodlots, such as agricultural areas, zero in on food sources that offer deer a high nutritional value, especially during periods of changing weather. When temperatures drop, for instance, deer are naturally attracted to corn because it raises body temperature. On the other hand, when the weather is warmer they prefer clover and alfalfa.

Although deer do not require watering holes in the true sense of the term, they will drink at specific spots along their normal travel routes. If you can find a watering area that's secluded and near heavy cover, you will increase your deer sightings immensely.

## Cover:

A deer's survival depends on cover that's secure from predators and hunting pressure. Locate cover areas that are hard to reach and generally inaccessible

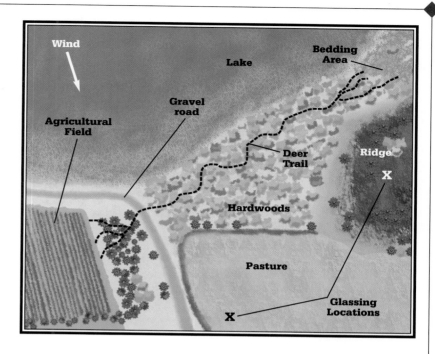

to all but the most persistent hunters. Look for the toughest, thickest, nastiest terrain. Generally, this means swamps, steep ledges and overgrown thickets. This is where the buck will be when the hunting pressure is on. Plan to set up along trails leading into and out of these areas.

## Terrain:

Use a topographic map to get a feel for the lay of the land and its natural and man-made obstructions. These barriers heavily influence how deer behave and travel. Deer are just like largemouth bass — you'll find them wherever there is natural structure to help conceal their movements.

Features to look for on topographic maps are saddles, natural funnels, flats and edges. Once you've located them, inspect them in person and figure out how to hunt them in the fall.

SADDLES — A saddle is a depression in a ridge running between two mountaintops. Bucks feel safe in saddles probably because the terrain breaks up their silhouettes. They also retreat to these areas during heavy winds.

FUNNELS — These lanes of terrain offer deer an easy "flow" through the woods, letting them travel from one

## LONG-RANGE SCOUTING

*Scout from a distance whenever possible. Set up with a spotting scope or binoculars where you can watch for deer movement without spooking deer or leaving scent (marked by x above). Frequent human intrusion can cause deer, especially bucks, to go nocturnal.*

place to another unnoticed. They are usually long, narrow corridors that begin at a high point and flow to a lower area. Check your topo map and you'll be able to find them without too much difficulty.

FLATS – Deer often use these benches, shelves or ledges (lying just below and parallel to ridgetops) as bedding areas. Bucks also make scrapelines across them.

EDGES – You'll find these on the fringes of swamps, where agricultural fields meet forests, or where stone walls border abandoned apple orchards. They can be anywhere one type of vegetation or terrain blends

into another. Deer are attracted to them because they usually offer food sources with cover nearby.

**Pressure:**

Try to figure out where other hunters will likely set up. Look for permanent tree stands, spent shells, ground blinds, marks on trees from climbing stands or screw-in steps – anything indicating the presence of other hunters. By knowing where other hunters will enter, hunt and exit an area, you can better place your stand along known escape routes or other trails that deer are likely to use.

Finally, make sure you don't over-scout

**HUNTING TIPS**

*Travel corridors will usually follow the cover in a terrain break such as a ravine, brushy fence row or field edge. A funnel along one of these travel routes is a hot spot for stand or blind placement.*

## FUNNELS

*Funnels – Cover in a funnel concentrates deer moving through from one area to another.*

## SADDLES

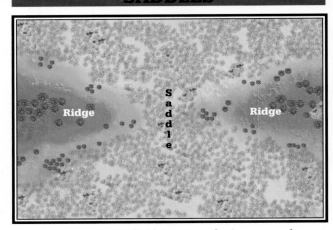

*Saddles – Deer avoid ridgetops, preferring to use depressions, called saddles, as crossings.*

## EDGES

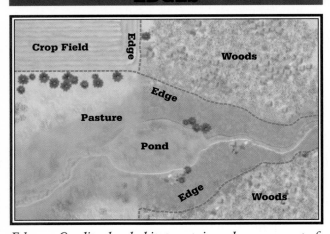

*Edges – Quality deer habitat contains a large amount of edge cover, which provides deer with both food and cover.*

## FLATS

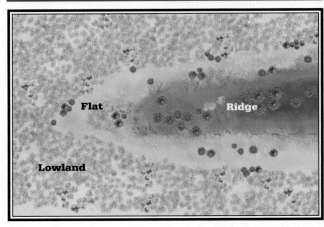

*Flats – Deer often use flats, also called benches or shelves, that lie just below ridgetops as bedding areas.*

your area. Even light pressure can make deer alter their movement patterns. End your scouting missions by September. Don't invade promising areas again until the season opens.

## Electronics:

TWO-WAY RADIOS – These are convenient, efficient, and can be used to get help if needed. Good for keeping in touch with hunting buddies.

HAND-HELD GPS UNITS – Getting lost is not a problem for some of us; getting found is. GPS can help you find your way back to the car, pinpoint choice locations in the dark, or find your way to any location you have referenced.

*GPS unit*

INFRARED DETECTOR – A hand-held infrared detector can help find downed game. A flashlight-sized unit can sense slight temperature differences in either wooded or open terrain.

HEARING DEVICES – Increase your game-hearing ability in the field without risking hearing damage. Units amplify high-frequency sounds like turkeys gobbling or leaves crackling under the hooves of a deer. Special features prevent amplification of gun-muzzle blasts.

LASER RANGEFINDERS – Affordable units are available for short-range yardage readings needed by bowhunters to 70 yards; rifle hunters may want to consider one that gives readings to a target up to 400 yards.

TRAIL MONITORS – Infrared monitors collect trail-use data. Units can record date and time of events at ranges of almost 100 feet, and some have optional camera connections.

**ACCURACY**

## SHOT DISTANCES

*Use the laser rangefinder to plot distances from your stand location to a rock, a tree or another object to help estimate shot distances.*

*Laser rangefinder*

*Limit intrusion by glassing from your vehicle*

# Patterning *Whitetails*

*By Dwight Schuh*

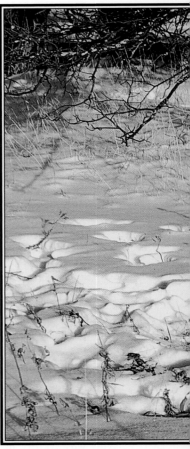

*Fresh scrapes show clearly in snow.*

To be in the right place at the right time for a whitetail buck, you must not only understand his home range movements but also analyze his travel patterns within that range. With a Ph.D. in wildlife science, white-tailed deer authority Dr. James Kroll offers the following prescription for patterning a buck.

## Scrapes:

In some regions, hunters plan their strategies around scrapes, but that doesn't work everywhere. According to Dr. Kroll, in areas with dense cover or low numbers of whitetails, using scrapes as a link between bucks and does is still important. But in regions with high deer populations, the need for scrapes has been reduced or even eliminated. The bucks may still instinctively scrape, but they don't always rely on scrapes to find does. The conclusion? Fresh scrapes tell you bucks are present but not necessarily where to place stands.

## Rubs:

From late summer on, bucks rub saplings to prepare for the rut. These rubs are concentrated around a buck's core areas and radiate from there along travel routes. Rubs can remain visible for years, forming lines that reliably identify bucks' travel corridors.

Even more meaningful are signpost rubs, which Dr. Kroll views as doors to a deer's life, the starting points for patterning a buck. Signposts normally appear on trees several inches in diameter in places readily visible to other deer, and they're rubbed year after year. While rubbing signposts, dominant bucks leave their scent, which, Dr. Kroll says, "has two specific functions: to inhibit subordinate bucks from breeding and to prime does for breeding. Most signposts mark core areas, the buck's centers of activity."

## Activity Centers:

Bedding areas, generally hidden in dense cover, are situated to assure deer good scenting conditions and escape routes in several directions. In addition to signposts, you'll often find many small rubs near the beds.

Staging areas are strips of heavy cover bordering fields and other open feeding sites where, Dr. Kroll

explains, deer often gather for an hour or more to scent-check and watch the field before venturing into the open. "A lot of social interaction takes place here, too," he says. "This is a gathering place where deer get to know each other." Staging areas are generally marked by obvious signposts as well as by numerous smaller rubs.

## Stand Locations:

Because bucks spend much time in staging and bedding areas, you'd think these would be the places to hunt, but Dr. Kroll believes otherwise. "I would never hunt these sanctuaries because they're 'high-knowledge areas' where bucks know every sight, sound and smell. You don't want to be in the destination point he's focusing on. Instead, I'd hunt the travel routes between these activity centers because these are areas of lower knowledge, where a deer is looking ahead to where he's going."

To find these travel routes, Dr. Kroll studies topographic maps. He particularly likes infrared aerial photos (available from government agencies) that show different timber and vegetation types,

wet and dry places, and other features influencing deer movement.

"Like bass, deer use structure," Dr. Kroll says. "Doe groups are associated with creek drainages, so start there. Then look for saddles between drainages and any changes in terrain, no matter how subtle. In flat country, a foot of elevation can be 'topography' because it makes a difference in vegetation."

In addition to vegetation lines, Dr. Kroll notes brush or timber strips that could channel deer between open areas, and he particularly likes corners where three types of vegetation — timber, a field and a slough, for example — come together. These intersections form ideal stand sites.

Having identified possible travel corridors, Dr. Kroll next scouts on the ground. All fresh sign catches his eye, but he relies heavily on rub lines as indicators of a buck's travel routes. And he shuns major trails. "A buck trail is usually subtle, not beat out like a doe trail," he says. "A buck will circle in thick brush downwind of the main trails. That's where you want your stand."

# Tips for Opening Day

*By Monte Burch*

*Advice from the experts on how to make your deer hunt successful.*

In most states, more bucks are taken on the first day than at any other time during the season. One reason for this is that the deer, not having been hunted all summer, are not feeling pressured, and are not on full alert for hunters. That changes once gunshots begin to go off and human scent permeates the woods. To give you your best shot at the best time, we asked eight seasoned hunters what they do on the opener.

## Scout for Food Sources:

*Ronnie Strickland, Haas Outdoors/ Mossy Oak*

"Scouting in many parts of the country, especially down South, mostly revolves around food sources. I begin long-distance scouting in late August, while crops are still in the field, using binoculars or spotting scopes from a good vantage point; many times, a vehicle. The whole purpose is to leave the deer undisturbed. Even the bigger bucks seem to show themselves around agricultural fields then. It may be right at dark, but they will show. Pick out landmarks where bucks continually enter fields; then move in and scout the area for precise stand locations.

"Scouting is an ongoing part of hunting. Once crops are gone, I focus on acorns. A knowledge of where the trees are is valuable. If you're in a new area, nothing beats legwork. You can't find those great out-of-the-way spots unless you're on your feet. I hunt the acorns until the bitter end, checking trees and moving to the freshest sign. Even when the rut kicks in, I stay on acorns if they're still available. Does will be eating them and the bucks will find the does. When acorns are gone, keep walking and find the current food source. It may be winter wheat or rye planted by farmers, but continue scouting the food."

From Mississippi, Strickland, 42, has been deer hunting 30 years. His favorite deer rifle is a 50-caliber in-line muzzleloader. His bow is a compound with graphite arrows, Simmons Landshark broadheads, no release.

## Use the Right Scents:

*Terry Rohm, Wellington/Tinks*

"Opening day here in Georgia is usually pretty warm. You need to reduce your body odor as much as possible because a deer's nose is his number-one defense. Use unscented soap, shampoo and laundry detergent. Don't use perfumes

at all. When you get into your stand, spray exposed skin and rub your face and hair with an odor neutralizer such as Non-Stink®. If it's really hot, you need to wash off your sweat with a cloth; I then put that cloth into a plastic bag because there's lots of odor and bacteria on it.

"It also helps to use a cover scent when you get to your tree stand. Early in the year I like to use buck urine. Because the rut is not on, the deer are not interested in rutting, but are interested in the social group communication. If a buck smells buck urine and thinks it's another buck, he comes in to get to know that buck. Tarsal gland [scent] works great, and it's something you can use for weeks if you take proper care of it. A lot of people try to use rut scent like Tink's

69® too early. The rut is not on, and it's just not right. Early in the season I don't use a lure to actually draw the deer in but to get them to stop, especially in bow season. I put lure on both sides of the trail, and when a buck comes down the trail and gets to that scent, he's going to smell it. When he stops, you need to shoot him, as that's your best opportunity."

Rohm, from Buckhead, Georgia, is 41, and has been hunting since he was 12 years old. His favorite bow is a Jennings Buckmaster with aluminum arrows; his favorite gun a Remington 25-06.

## Decoy Them into Range:

*Dave Berkley, Feather Flex Decoys*

"Last year we discovered that although deer will approach a single decoy

*Deer prefer feeding in fields under low-light conditions (above).*

## DON'T GET BUGGED

*Mosquitos and gnats can be brutal during warm, early-season hunting. Wearing a full-screen face mask keeps them out of your face and eyes.*

cautiously, when you put multiples out, caution is thrown to the wind and they just barge right in. I had only one old doe get cautious last year on approaching a multiple set. Bucks just absolutely, tail-down, head-up, come right on in."

*Spooked buck*

Berkley has also been experimenting with using turkey decoys as confidence decoys for bowhunting whitetails. "I carry five or six and make a little flock. A deer will not move or feed through a flock of feeding turkeys, because the birds will chase him off. They do pay attention to the turkeys, but will always skirt around them. I steer deer with my flock, making them go the way I want, right by my stand."

Berkley, 50, has been deer hunting since he was 16. He lives in Louisiana, and is primarily a bowhunter. He hunts with a High Country bow, Beman arrows, Elk Country broadheads and a Pro release.

## Call Them In:

*David Hale, Knight & Hale Game Calls*

"You need to match your calling on opening day to the timing and geographical region you're hunting. If it's bow season, in most places that's the first of October. You're basically looking at feeding and bedding periods, with the rest of the day wasted. Get as close to those areas as you can, then use contact sounds. They're not a lot different from the grunting sounds you'll use in the rut, except you're more aggressive during the rut. Here you're trying to get their attention and

say 'I'm a deer, I'm over here,' and they come out of curiosity. As the season progresses and the deer become more mobile, do more calling. There's also more opportunities during the course of the day.

"In those areas where the peak of the rut occurs on opening day of gun season, you need to do as much calling as possible because those deer are in a search mode and they're likely to walk into your realm of calling any hour of the day.

"For those states that open gun season during the post-rut, as do many northern states, you need to spend your time calling around areas where you've seen a lot of sign. Bucks are often easier to call during this time because they're searching for does again. It may be the best time to call."

David Hale is from Kentucky, 51 years old, and has been hunting whitetails since age 14. He uses a 30-06 deer rifle and a PSE Whitetail Hunter bow, Simmons broadheads, ACC carbon arrows and shoots with a release. "I've got to have every advantage in the world," he says.

## Stay All Day:

*Peter J. Fiduccia, Outdoorsman's Edge Book Club*

"We hunt about 55 minutes outside the heart of Manhattan, in New York. It's basically farm country — cows, apples and corn — and we have a fair amount of pressure. We have a lot of people coming up out of the city as well as lots of people who live in the area and hunt. You have the occasional buck that's killed the first hour or two in the morning, but we find that on opening day, most of the deer are killed around 9:30 A.M. and 1:30 P.M. My basic advice is to go into the woods with enough clothes, food and drink so you don't have to leave your stand or come out during the midday period.

"It used to be a guy could go into the woods on opening day and there were only a few archers who had been chasing deer around before that. Nowadays there are so many archers, especially in this area, that by the time firearms season opens the deer already know they're being hunted hard. So opening day isn't the magic time that it used to be, when you might catch a buck off guard as he's sneaking back to his bed. We find that if you stay in the woods, and in that one stand, the entire day, eventually a deer moved by somebody winds up coming by your stand."

Fiduccia, from New York, just turned 50. His favorite gun is a 280 Remington, his bow is a Golden Eagle with aluminum arrows and Satellite Titan broadheads, and he uses a release.

## Learn the New Patterns:

*Tony Knight, Knight Rifles*

"Make sure all your equipment is in shape, your rifle is sighted in, you've worked up the correct load and you have the accessories needed. One thing you need to remember is, on opening day of gun season, the bucks won't follow the same pattern they did earlier during archery season. All of a sudden, all those flashlights start coming through the woods on opening morning and it's a shock to them. But if you're lucky, somebody is going to drive one by your stand. Although I'm sure it's more efficient to stay in your stand, I like to hunt the first couple of hours or so from a tree, then get down about 10:00 A.M. and do some still-hunting. I take a cushion and walk a bit, then sit quite a while.

"There's often another opening day, the special muzzleloader season in many states, and it's usually after the normal gun season. Hunting is usually a lot tougher because of the pressure the deer have seen. During that time, still-hunting, and watching food sources early and late in the morning, will be productive. You will have to do a lot of walking, looking and some stirring up with drives."

Knight, from Iowa, is 51 and has been hunting for 30 years. His favorite gun? A Knight in-line muzzleloader.

## Hunt Escape Routes:

*Brad Harris, Lohman Game Calls*

"On opening day of gun season, I like to position myself where I can see a long way so I can cover as much property as possible. I try to set up where several fingers, or two or three ridges, might meet in a saddle, places where I can get as much deer traffic as possible. But I won't hunt those areas after the first couple of days, because they're too open.

"If I'm hunting public land and I know pressure is going to come from different parking areas, then I'll set up along escape routes from those areas. I'll get into the thickest spots where deer will try to seek refuge when they feel pressure from other hunters that morning. I'll set up in places where it's necked-down — again, saddles — but thick lines of edge or timber where they travel when spooked."

Harris, from Missouri, is 40 years old and has been deer hunting since 1970. His favorite rifle is a 270, favorite bow a Golden Eagle Pro Revolution. He likes Easton arrows and Satellite Titan broadheads, and he doesn't use a release. Harris used to bowhunt on opening day of the gun season, but for the past few years he's used a gun so he can hunt with his teenaged son, who took a record whitetail buck scoring 192$\frac{3}{8}$ gross last season.

## Take a Smart Stand:

*Jay Cassell, Contributing Editor at* Outdoor Life *magazine*

"Where you place your tree stand is critical. I look for a tree that overlooks a deer runway, or where a couple of trails cross. I scout during the preseason to make sure those runways are being used, then place my tree stand 10 or 15 yards back from the intersection of the trails. I try to place it in, or in front of, a hemlock so my silhouette is broken up. With dense cover behind me, deer probably won't see me draw my bow or raise my rifle. If I have to hang my tree stand in a tree that's out in the open, I try to put it on the side of the tree opposite the trails. I never go so high that I feel queasy, but I do like to be at least 15 feet up. You really need to set up your tree stand and then see what the view is like. You may not want to go too high because in some situations deer will be able to see you from far away. For instance, on one hill that I hunt, I put my tree stand too high and deer were seeing me from 200 yards away. Last year I moved the seat down about two feet and now they can't see me until they're right up on me.

"Always use a safety belt when you go into a tree stand. Climbing trees is serious stuff; I've heard and read about too many people either killed or injured from falling out of stands. It can happen to you."

Cassell, from New York, is 45, and has been deer hunting for 20 years. He has used a 30-06 Browning BAR for the past 10 years, but is switching to an Ultra Light Arms 30-06 this year. For bowhunting he uses a Golden Eagle Evolution bow, Easton 2117 aluminum arrows, Satellite Titan broadheads and Scott release.

*Good tree stand location is vital to deer hunting success.*

# The *Magnificent Seven*

*By Monte Burch*

*Super sites for deer stands.*

**S**ome deer-stand locations produce bucks season after season, while others produce sporadically, if at all. What makes a certain location better than others? Several factors: topography, vegetation, land use, hunting pressure and breeding habits. Following are the seven best deer-stand sites in the woods, with details on how to find them, how to set up once you locate them, and how to hunt them.

# 1 Saddles:

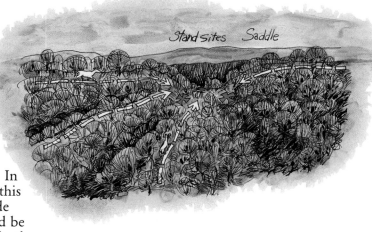

A saddle or notch in a ridge is an excellent site for a stand. If several ridges join, and there's a saddle at the junction, that's even better. Bucks running the ridge can drop off either side at the first hint of danger, as these notches offer concealment. In fact, the only way to see deer in this situation is if you're on either side of the ridge crown. Stands should be located to one side, not directly in the saddle, so you're not skylined.

# 2 Brush-Choked Draws:

A brush-choked draw or ravine, especially in open prairie or sparsely wooded country, is also a good spot. As with saddles, a location where two or more draws come together will have even more use. Deer not only travel through the cover afforded by ravines, they bed in them as well. The head of the draw is normally the best location for a stand, but again, situate yourself off to one side. If you find more deer trails on one side of the draw than the other, place your bow stand on the side with more trails, your rifle stand on the opposite.

**T I P S**

### Dealing with the Wind

*Regardless of how great a specific area might be, specific stand location should be determined by wind direction. Ideally, you should have several possible stand positions around the site to allow for different wind directions. When hunting, approach your stand from downwind, checking around it for deer use before you get there, particularly in the afternoon. I use a piece of surveyor's tape tied to a stick as a mini windsock. Using it, I keep an eye on the wind and choose my stand accordingly. I also have some thread tied to each of my stands and change sites if I see the wind direction has changed.*

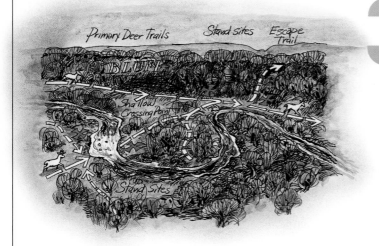

Primary Deer Trails    Stand sites    Escape Trail
BLUFF
Shallow Crossing Point
Stand Sites

## 3 Funnels:

A creek or river that runs up against a steep hill or bluff will squeeze trails into a small area, creating a funnel that game must pass through. Setting up a stand that overlooks these compressed trails, or a shallow area where deer cross the river, is always a good choice — especially if you can determine when deer use the trails and from which direction they normally approach. In open country, look for woodlots connected by treelines or fencerows, then set up so you can intercept deer moving between bedding and feeding areas.

**THINK AHEAD**

## ALL DAY

Plan to spend all day on stand especially when there is heavy hunting pressure or during the rut. Bucks looking for does or being pushed by other hunters may pass by your location at any time during the day.

## 4 Clearings & Clear-cuts:

In heavily wooded areas, a change in vegetation is always a good spot to look for deer. In fairly open woods, look for pockets of heavy brush, as bucks like to hide there when hunting pressure is on. If mast-producing trees are near such pockets, deer will bed in the brush and move out to feed. Overgrown clear-cuts are also great spots because they provide food and cover. A clearing or old logging road in any type of woods can also have potential.

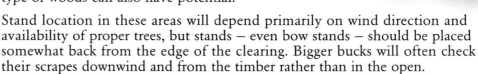

Stand site    Scrapes    Stand site
Mast-Producing Trees
Clearing
Prevailing Wind    Old Logging Road

Stand location in these areas will depend primarily on wind direction and availability of proper trees, but stands — even bow stands — should be placed somewhat back from the edge of the clearing. Bigger bucks will often check their scrapes downwind and from the timber rather than in the open.

## 5 Feeding & Bedding Areas:

Although field edges may be littered with tracks, most big bucks don't feed until after dark and are rarely seen in open fields unless they're chasing does. A white-oak acorn grove, or even a single oak in timber, however, will always attract bucks, often trophies. Scout your hunting area, try to determine both the feeding and bedding areas, then locate your stand between the two. Unless greatly disturbed, deer will stick to their daily routines and use certain trails in the morning, others at night (depending upon the area, they may use the same trails). Deer will generally feed in the open fields at night, then head back to heavy cover in the early morning, where they will bed for the day. Locate evening stands closer to the bedding area and morning stands closer to the feed field.

Feeding area (crop field)    Morning Stand site    Evening Stand site    Bedding area (dense thicket)
Open Woods

## 6 Escape Routes:

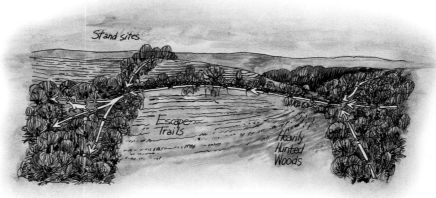

Used by deer when pressured, escape routes are often found in saddles or funnels, usually with heavy vegetation. Be in a stand along an escape route early in the morning on opening day, before the woods become full of hunters, and you're almost guaranteed to see deer. I've hunted one such spot opening morning for 10 years, and it always has deer traffic about a half hour after the first shots ring out. A brushy draw in a field on a heavily hunted farm to the east leads to a brushy hillside above a river that borders a public hunting area to the south. My stand is on the brushy hillside, at the juncture where draw meets river.

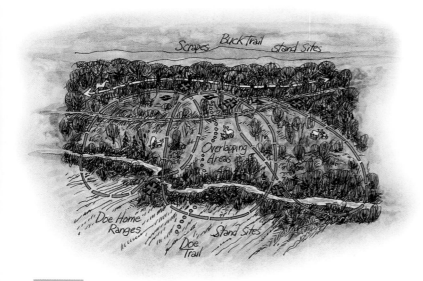

## 7 Breeding Zones:

Deer breed in certain areas determined by topography, vegetation and doe home ranges. These home ranges are often as small as 40 acres, and does will drive other deer away from them, with their daughters establishing their own areas nearby. Each doe has a core fawning ground within her home range. An area with good food and cover will often contain overlapping doe home ranges.

When looking for a breeding zone, search for a fairly open area with good escape cover and numerous entrance and exit trails. Clearings in timbered areas, secluded field edges and open creekbottoms are good examples. Multiple scrapes, with at least one that's active, are dead giveaways of prime zones.

---

# TIPS

### Land Use & Hunting Pressure

*If land uses change, so will deer patterns. A new logging operation, a cropland harvested or plowed up, cattle being turned into an area to graze: All of these can halt deer activity in the area around your stand. Last-minute scouting is the only way to know what's going on.*

*If land-use patterns remain the same at your stand site but deer activity drops off anyway, you might be overhunting it. Big bucks pattern your use of an area as quickly as you do theirs. Once they know you're hunting their territory, they'll use it only nocturnally, as I've learned through studies with infrared trail-timers. Prevent this by having several stand sites available, so you can rotate your stand activity.*

*The best still-hunters plan each step carefully.*

# The Still-Hunting Advantage

*By Jay Cassell*

**T**he buck never knew I was there. I had been pussyfooting down an old logging trail, pausing every five yards or so, stopping every 20. I was standing next to a large hemlock, my body partially obscured by branches, watching the road in front of me, when I saw movement off to the right. A deer was moving down a trail that intersected the logging road 40 yards ahead.

Head down, nose to the ground, the buck was obviously following the scent of a doe. Caution was the last thing on his mind. When he reached the logging road, he skidded to a stop, turned and looked right at me. Too late. I took him with one shot.

Still-hunting. It's a highly effective way of hunting deer, especially if you do it at the right time, in the right place, the right way.

## When:

Much depends upon the weather. On still days, with crunchy leaves or icy snow covering the ground, still-hunting is out of the question. No matter how quiet you try to be, you'll still make too much noise and spook any deer way before you can get within gun range. Better to remain in a tree stand on still days, and still-hunt on windy days, when gusts conceal your leaf crunching, or on damp or rainy days, when ground cover is wet and won't make noise when stepped on. Deer also tend to bed down on rainy and especially windy days, so your best chance of getting a shot at a buck under such conditions is to go find one, on foot, quietly.

## Where:

No matter what the weather, I like to still-hunt when I'm in new territory. While I prefer a tree stand when the situation is right, I don't have a clue where to put up a stand when I'm in unfamiliar country. Still-hunting lets me learn the property, plus it gives me a better chance at a deer than just putting up a stand in any old tree.

In damp or windy conditions, when deer are probably bedded down, I head to the thickest cover I can find. Rhododendron stands, hemlock groves, cedar swamps, thickets, steep ledges; anyplace a buck is likely to bed down is where I'll go. When hunting such spots, wear camo if the law allows, and move slower than slow.

Deer pick these spots not only because they're sheltered, but also because they can watch for approaching danger.

When hunting tough-to-reach cover, pay special attention to the wind. Even if you're wearing a cover scent that's consistent with the area's vegetation, moving into an area with the wind at your back dictates that you stop and figure an alternative route. The brush may be ridiculously thick, or the ledges perilously steep, but common sense says you should try to circle around and approach from downwind. Being lazy and just barging ahead anyway will only ensure that you won't see deer.

## How:

This may sound like a cliché, but it's true: If you think you're going too fast, you are. Serious still-hunting means going painfully slow, so slow that it's almost boring. But you're doing this for a number of reasons. With each step you take, you have a different perspective of the woods. A bedded buck can come into view with just one or two steps. Take five or six, and that buck will detect your movement and be history before you even know he's there.

You're also moving slowly because you want to be quiet. Take each step carefully. Watch where you're putting your feet. If you suspect there might be a stick under the wet leaves you're about to step on, put your foot down slowly. Gradually increase the pressure,

## SNEAK-HUNTING

*Sneak-hunting is the ultimate challenge in deer hunting. To be successful requires patience, woodsmanship skills, some luck and a consistent wind.*

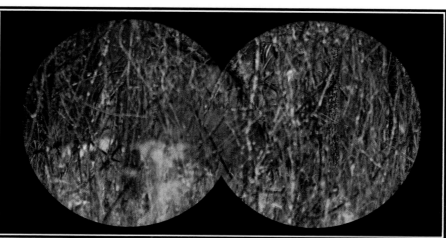

*View with naked eye*      *Use of binoculars will reveal details*

putting your weight first on your heel, then on the rest of your foot. As you go, if you can put your foot on a rock that won't tip, on moss, on snow – anything that you're certain won't make noise – do it. If you're in an area where you know your footsteps will be silent, then don't watch your feet. Instead, watch the woods in front of you and around you. I'm not talking woods that are 25 yards in front of you, either; rather, 100 yards or more. That's where you're likely to see a buck, not close up. Train yourself to look as far as you can see, and you'll start spotting deer you wouldn't have seen otherwise.

As you move through a given patch of woods, be aware of where the large, silhouette-breaking trees are located. Pause by them. The last thing you want to do is pause out in the open, because that's exactly when a buck is going to come walking into view and see you. Pause by trees, as I did

on that logging road, boulders, blowdowns, anything to break up your silhouette. And do it no matter where you are; even if you think you're in an area where you know a buck won't be, still-hunt carefully, and pause by large objects.

**Be Ready:**

Three years ago I was hunting in New York's Catskill Mountains. I was way down the mountain, hunting virtually inaccessible ledges. With a lot of hunting pressure up top, I figured deer would be down low, away from the crowds. It was nearing the end of the season, there was snow on the ground, it was late afternoon. The snow was somewhat crunchy, so I was moving extra carefully, placing my feet on rocks whenever feasible.

Dropping down to another ledge, I stopped next to a boulder. Generally when I stop, I don't move for at least five minutes, usually 10. Just as I was

*Plan your still-hunt so you'll pass through areas known to contain deer, and choose several stand sites with sufficient cover to hide your presence. In the example shown, the hunter's first stand site was against a wide tree, which he used to break up his outline. After an hour or so, he moved to the next site, where he sat on the ground, disguising his profile by leaning against a tall stump. About two hours later, he moved to the next site, where he took up an elevated stand by placing a board in the "Y" of the tree. An hour later, the hunter took a new stand at the base of a fallen tree, hiding in its uplifted root system. For his final stand of the day, the hunter slipped in between three trees that gave him cover from several directions.*

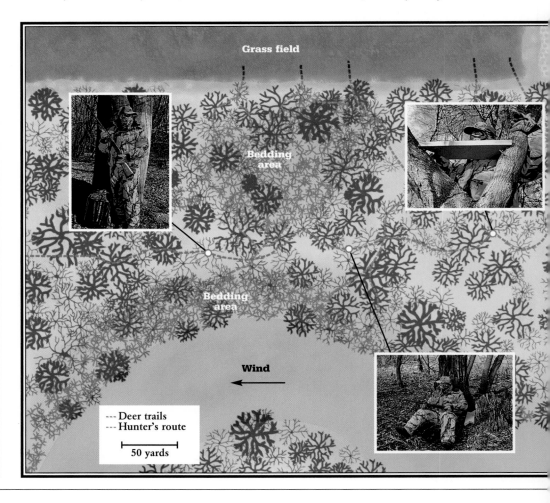

Grass field

Bedding area

Bedding area

Wind

--- Deer trails
--- Hunter's route

50 yards

about to end my break and move another 25 yards or so, I heard something crunching off to my right. Sure enough, a doe and yearling appeared, moving along my ledge. To my surprise, they came to within 10 yards of me, then stopped and started to paw the ground, looking for food. They didn't see me at all. And while I was tempted to quietly say *Boo*, I stayed silent and motionless. I wanted to see what would happen.

What happened was that I heard more crunching off to my right. Now antlers came up over the lip of the ledge. It was a 7-pointer, just 30 yards away. He looked at the does and then froze, his widening eyes riveted on me. He had me, but he didn't move; obviously the presence of the does so close to me had him confused. What would he do? I figured I'd better do something, because he'd probably bolt any second. Ever so slowly, I started to raise my rifle. If I could get it just halfway up

to my shoulder, I could take a snapshot and maybe get him.

Naturally, it didn't work that way. The retractable scope cap snapped on the zipper of my camo jacket. Both the doe and yearling heard it and looked right at me; then all hell broke loose. Throwing the gun to my shoulder, I looked through the scope and immediately saw brown. But it wasn't the buck! It was the yearling, running to my left, blocking my view of the buck. And within seconds it was over, as all three deer disappeared over the edge of the ledge. I took no shot at the buck, as the only shot I had, at the last split second, was a running kidney shot. Too risky, in that situation.

Lesson learned? Whenever I stop somewhere now, I never, never, hold my gun low on my body, no matter how tired I am. Port arms is always my rule now. And so is that time-honored piece of advice: Always be ready, because you never know.

## HUNTING TIPS

# COVERING SOUNDS

*Suburban deer hunters may time their movement to the covering sounds of passing cars, trucks, trains or airplanes.*

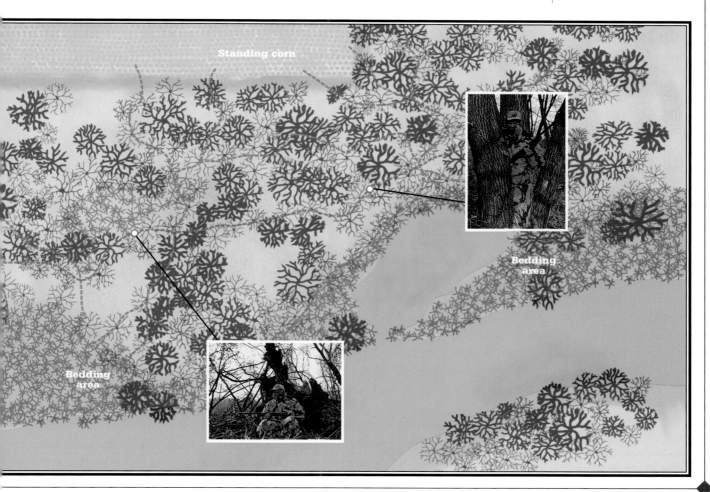

Standing corn

Bedding area

Bedding area

# Glass & Stalk

*By Don Oster*

*It's the epitome of true hunting skills. You must search for, locate and move in on your deer.*

**B**en Miller and I were on a high ridge overlooking a large canyon somewhere in the Black Hills in the northeast corner of Wyoming. Our eyes were glued to our binoculars. I can't be too clear about our exact location because we took a twisting, turning route along a maze of old logging roads and forest service trails to get on top. Once there, we could glass several intersecting canyons on both sides of the main ridge.

Miller's "I see one" jolted me out of an in-the-glasses trance. Sure enough, a lone doe was moving across the lower part of the canyon. Noting her trail as she climbed up and crossed a saddle connecting our ridge to an adjacent

*Glass all terrain patiently*

one, we went back to glassing. In only a few minutes, more movement along the trail revealed the buck we were looking for. No question, he was on the doe's trail, moving at a steady, purposeful gait. Even though the distance was several hundred yards, his antlers stood out.

Without hesitation we both jumped up and started for the saddle, determined to intercept the big whitetail. Our jog along the top of the ridge wasn't bad, but the descent was tricky. It turned into a helter-skelter stalk down the ridge, trying to hurry, while not making excess noise or dislodging rocks as we went. Reaching the base of the incline, we selected an ambush spot about 150 yards from where the main trail crossed the saddle. I had just resumed normal breathing when the 10-pointer appeared, his nose to the ground, following the doe. He looked for all the world like a bird dog tracking a quail. When the buck stopped, I placed my scope's crosshairs on his rib cage and squeezed the trigger on my .264. He never knew what hit him.

### Glass & Stalk Basics:

Glassing and stalking is a good method to use on whitetails in any open country, including agricultural areas mixed with sloughs, woods and draws, mountain foothills, canyons and broken country in the West, where whitetails live along wooded creeks and rivers. Watching from a high point with binoculars or spotting scope to locate deer feeding, bedded or moving about may be the only option for whitetail hunting in the rugged hill country of Texas. Coues deer in southern Arizona and New Mexico are usually spotted from a long distance, then stalked to within gun range. Any place in whitetail range where there are wide-open spaces and vantage points high enough to see down into cover is good for glassing and stalking.

Study your hunting area to see if you're missing a bet by not using this method. If there are ridges, hilltops,

rimrock or points that overlook feeding locations, bedding areas, trails, travel corridors, funnels or cover edges, you've got possibilities. If the terrain allows either shooting from the vantage points or planned stalks to within range, you've got to add this method to your repertoire of hunting techniques.

By glassing and stalking, you can hunt large areas with a small expense of energy and you can cover heavy deer-use areas with only your eyes, leaving no scent or other sign of your intrusion. You can also observe deer that are usually undisturbed and map their patterns even when a stalk or shot won't work at the moment. Glass and stalk can lead you to use other techniques. If you repeatedly observe a big buck feeding at dawn in the edge of a crop field, set up a stand or blind there and he's likely to come by the next morning. Glassing and stalking when deer activity increases during the rut can also create some opportunities at big bucks.

### Equipment:

Top-quality optics are essential to effective glassing and stalking. The basic tools are binoculars, a spotting scope and rifle scope. Binoculars are generally used to cover wide expanses of territory. The best binoculars for this technique are full-sized models that can be worn comfortably around the neck in the 7x35 to 10x40 range. More powerful binoculars are too hard to hold still for effective glassing. Pocket-sized binoculars are popular because of their light weight, but most of these models do not perform well under low-light conditions such as those found at dawn and dusk.

A spotting scope has a longer optical reach, which helps you zero in on a buck you've found with the glasses. Using the extra power of the scope, you can size up his trophy potential by counting points, estimating the mass and horn spread. Always use a tripod on a spotting scope; you simply cannot hold a high-power optic still enough to zero in on game. A 20x,

**ACCURACY**

## KNOW THE ARC

*To make the long shots that are some-times necessary when glassing and stalking, you must know your rifle's trajectory. Shooting at measured long ranges is the only sure way to learn your bullet's flight path.*

30x or 40x fixed-power scope works well for most deer-hunting situations; however, a zoom or variable-power scope has some advantages. With the zoom, you can scope a wide area at low power, then increase the magnification for a closer look.

Sometimes glass and stalk becomes glass and shoot because the terrain or cover will not permit a stalk to closer range. The unseen steep canyon or open field may necessitate that the shot be taken from there or passed. In these circumstances, a scoped, flat-shooting rifle sighted in for long-range shots is a must. A variable-power scope providing a bright, sharp sight picture complements a rifle with long-range capability. Shots through a hole in brush at 100 yards or a 300-yard shot across a canyon may be necessary. A variable-power scope set at 8 or 9x helps increase the chances of a good shot.

The glass-and-stalk hunter using a bow, shotgun or muzzleloader accepts the challenge of stalking to within the limited range of the weapon. The stalk must be carefully planned and executed to be successful. Quiet clothing, soft, padded shoes or sneakers and as much outer camo as the law allows can help in the final stages of a close-in sneak.

### How to Glass & Stalk:

Tony Oliva, a former Minnesota Twins player, had a simple approach to hitting: "See ball, hit ball." Glass and stalk appears as simple: see buck, sneak in,

shoot buck. This technique does get more involved because of variables in terrain and cover and deer that don't always behave as we predict.

First select one or more vantage points on hilltops, ridges, canyon rims or points overlooking areas frequently used by deer. Elevation is key; the higher the better, since you want to be able to see down into cover. Do not skyline yourself; use available natural cover or terrain as a background. Keep movement slow and minimal. Be on your first vantage point at first light. Scan the entire area, but concentrate first on crop fields and other open feeding areas. On subsequent scans, as the light improves, check field edges, fencerows, ravines and other shadowed places.

You will only see an entire deer when one is standing in a wide-open place such as a field or clearing. At most times you will be looking for a piece of a deer — the horizontal line of a back, wag of a tail, flick of an ear or slight head movement. Sun glinting off an antler tip should really get your attention. Concentrate on any spot that shows even the slightest movement until you're certain it is not a deer. Birds, rabbits and other animals can be deceptive; make sure not to overlook any possibility.

If you have more than one vantage point, change locations as soon as you have thoroughly looked over an area. Move to another place along the most concealed, quietest route. Again, do

## SIGHT-IN

*A ballistic table (below) for selected factory loaded cartridges is a starting point for sighting in as you prepare for long-range shooting. Make adjustments as you test your cartridge in your gun.*

| | Bullet Size (grams) | Muzzle Velocity (feet per second) | Sight-In Yardage (yards) | Trajectory (yards) | | | |
|---|---|---|---|---|---|---|---|
| | | | | 100 | 200 | 300 | 400 |
| 25-06 Remington | 120 | 2900 | 240 | +2.7 | +1.9 | -4.7 | -18.0 |
| 270 Winchester | 140 | 2900 | 243 | +2.7 | +1.9 | -4.3 | -17.0 |
| 280 Remington | 150 | 2800 | 234 | +2.7 | +1.7 | -5.4 | -20.0 |
| 7mm Remington Mag. | 150 | 2900 | 242 | +2.7 | +1.9 | -4.4 | -17.0 |
| 30-06 | 165 | 2800 | 234 | +2.7 | +1.7 | -5.4 | -20.0 |
| 300 Winchester Mag. | 165 | 3000 | 250 | +2.6 | +2.0 | -3.6 | -15.0 |

not move along the skyline. Change locations slightly to get a different sight angle into the cover. Bedded deer are especially hard to see. However, a buck will occasionally get up, urinate and move to another bedding location.

When you spot a buck you want, first take time to carefully observe what he's doing. If he's bedded, reference the spot by some physical landmark. If the deer is moving, try to determine his speed and travel direction and pick a likely ambush spot. Plan the stalk along a route where you can be completely concealed by terrain features or cover. Be aware of wind direction; take pains to stay downwind from the target's approach. Reference your planned route by landmarks and physical features, recognizing that the terrain will look different up close than it did from above. Be prepared to crawl to reach a shooting range and position.

Once your target is in sight, get into a solid, comfortable shooting position. Use a tree, rock or other object that will provide a solid rest. Some hunters have a bipod installed on the rifle's fore-end; others carry crossed sticks to make a rest. When the target is within your shooting-confidence range, align the sights and place the shot.

# Whitetail Tactics for *Three Stages of the* Rut

*By Peter J. Fiduccia*

*How to hunt smart from opening day to season's end.*

**M**ost hunters know that their best chance of getting a buck is during the rut, when deer — males in particular — abandon their cautious ways in their urge to mate. What many *don't* know is that the rut lasts a lot longer than a few weeks in November, and that it's triggered by decreasing daylight — photoperiodism — which increases the levels of testosterone in bucks and estrogen in does. The hunter who knows about the different phases of the rut, and what occurs during each, can formulate an effective, season-long hunting plan.

## Pre-Rut:

The first rut, called the pre-rut or false rut, usually begins the first week of October and ends by mid-month. Most mature does go into a brief estrous cycle at this time. Since this early rut usually occurs during bow season,

bucks come across relatively few hunters in the woods and are eager to locate does throughout the day. Therefore, they respond to tactics that they will ignore in only a few weeks. Capitalize on this by using two types of scent: a deer tail decoy and a deer call.

## Instinctive Behavior:

Where legal and safe, take the tail of a deer and sprinkle it with buck urine and estrous urine. (I use this tactic only during archery season.) Thread 30 yards of string (any color but white) through a hole at the base of the tail. Hang the tail from a branch about 20 yards from your stand, at the height of a doe's rump (24 to 32 inches). Unravel the string from the tail back to your stand. Tie the remaining string end around your foot (or forearm, if you are in a ground stand). Twitch the tail every so often while making a soft, long blat on a deer call.

*Bucks are ready to breed immediately after shedding their velvet, which generally happens in late August. Most does, however, don't enter their first heat or estrous cycle this early. Frustrated bucks begin acting out rutting behavior anyway. They become aggressive toward one another; they spar with saplings and brush; and they begin to break away from bachelor groups. This behavior serves not only to establish a pecking order; it also stimulates does into entering their first heat cycle.*

*Two evenly matched competitors may fight for a half hour to settle breeding rights (opposite).*

This will attract bucks through their senses of smell, sight and hearing. Bucks respond because the rut has just started and they have few apprehensions. Just the twitching of the scent-laden tail is often enough to make a buck charge out of cover to investigate what he believes to be a hot doe. Calling along with this can attract bucks that are out of visual range, but have picked up the pheromones emanating from the tail.

*Buck breeding a doe*

## Primary Rut:

By counting 28 days from the last signs of the pre-rut (around October 15), you can determine when the start of the second rut, called the primary or main rut, normally occurs. This second cycle, when most does are bred, begins around November 10 and extends through November 25. Deer experience the most hunting pressure during the main rut since it coincides with most states' firearms seasons. Although bucks still chase does during this time, it doesn't take them long to wise up and begin breeding does nocturnally. Even though many hunters say that bucks go completely nocturnal at this time, they can still be encouraged to respond. The trick is to use different tactics. Most hunters go on stand before light, hunt until midmorning, return to camp for lunch, then go back to their stands from around 2:00 P.M. until dark. Bucks pick up on these patterns and adjust their movements accordingly. They realize that to search for does safely, they must do so between 10:00 A.M. and 1:00 P.M. — when many hunters are out of the woods.

## Get Agitated:

Unorthodox but effective, "rub-grunting" combines the pheromones of agitative scents that are common at this time of the year: tarsal and buck urine. The pheromones stimulate bucks into responding. During the day bucks generally wind-check their scrapes from the protection of cover. If a buck picks up an aroma he likes, such as that from a doe, he usually waits until she leaves the scrape and enters cover before he pursues her. If he smells what he thinks is a competitive buck, however, he often charges from cover to confront him.

To rub-grunt, locate a fresh primary scrape (two to three feet in diameter, moist, bare earth). Set up 10 to 30 yards from it. Don't worry about making too much noise. I find that creating natural noises (snapping twigs, making soft grunts, shaking surrounding brush) on my way to the stand helps to set up the illusion of a buck invading another buck's primary scrape. Begin by pawing the leaves

away from your stand, methodically and purposefully, as if you were a buck making a scrape.

Next, deposit a combination of tarsal and buck urine scents onto the bare earth. Do not use too much, as a buck may be bedded down fairy close by. Overusing scent could alarm rather than attract him. While depositing the scent, make three to five burplike grunts. These grunts must be very short, to simulate the sounds of a frustrated buck — erp...erp...erp. Blow the grunt sequence every three to five minutes, starting from when you paw out the leaves and disperse the scent.

Now comes the coup de grace. Take a small "Y" or forked-horn antler and vigorously rub a nearby sapling. Remember, to call deer effectively, you want to create not only the entire illusion, but a realistic one as well. Bucks that rub saplings do so in a deliberate way. They rub their antlers several times, stop, sniff and lick the sapling or branch, then begin rubbing again. So take a break every eight or 10 rubs, as opposed to constantly rubbing. After rubbing the tree bare of bark, hesitate for a few minutes, then make a series of grunts. Shake the sapling aggressively, then start all over again.

Bucks are attracted not only by the competitive scent of the tarsal and buck urine, but also by the sounds and sights you have created with the scraped leaves, rubbed antlers and shaking brush. Be ready for bucks to appear any time when doing this.

## Post-Rut:

The post- or late rut occurs about 28 days from the onset of the primary rut. When a doe comes into estrus during this time, she seeks seclusion from the family group. This solitude, and the resulting lack of competing estrous pheromones, is what makes the does a magnet to bucks. Making her the center of attention is nature's way of assuring that this late-season doe will get bred. Many times, a single doe will attract a number of bucks at the same time.

## Competitive Tactics:

Employ these during the post-rut. One method uses a commercially manufactured scent that combines doe-in-estrus scent mixed with the urine of an immature buck (2½ years old or younger), and it is deadly in areas that does frequent. Apply the scent to a boot pad and walk along the fringes of a main deer trail, heading toward your stand. Once you are 10 to 30 yards from your stand, walk a circle around your location and remove the pad. Sprinkle the sole of your boot with a couple of drops of estrous scent and go directly to your stand (this will help cover the human odor on your boots).

To complete the strategy, make several long, whining doe bleats. This imitates what occurs in the woods: Does that have not been bred announce their "readiness" by walking through the woods while emitting whiny bleats, trying to attract bucks.

By making a mock estrous trail, you create first-come, first-served competition. A buck traveling down your mock scent trail will smell not only the doe's estrus, but the aroma of an immature, competitive buck as well. His reaction will be to trot along the trail looking for the doe, thinking it will be easy to run off the younger buck. Your estrous bleats serve to further stimulate the buck. Be prepared, as most bucks will be moving quickly. They may trot past your stand several times, trying not only to zero in on the doe, but to locate the other buck as well.

**WHITETAIL FACTS**

*To perpetuate the species, nature enables the breeding cycle of white-tailed deer to continue for as long as there are does to be bred and bucks that have their antlers. Recent studies in New York, for example, prove that deer breed into January, February, even March, meaning there is, in effect, an eight-month breeding cycle. (Understand that, and use it to your advantage).*

*Buck searching for a receptive doe during the post-rut period*

# Deer Tricks
## (wind, rattling, scent)

*By Peter J. Fiduccia*

*Serious hunters know that whitetails depend on their senses of hearing, sight and smell to survive. They also know how to manipulate those senses to their advantage.*

Deer that are "on alert" use all their senses simultaneously (right).

# W I N D

*Testing wind-blown scent*

*The key to successful hunting is knowing how to read and interpret air currents.*

**N**othing plays a more important role in a buck's daily existence and survival than his sense of smell. He may on occasion ignore danger signals he sees or hears, but he will never disregard those he smells. White-tailed deer depend on their sense of smell, and use even the slightest air currents to pinpoint danger, water and food sources and estrous does. Therefore, the hunter who pays attention to wind direction is the one who will see, and ultimately shoot, the most deer.

Meteorologists define wind as air in horizontal motion relative to the surface of the earth. It can be broken down further into ascending and descending currents. Wind normally picks up during the day, as the temperature increases, and slows in the late afternoon around sunset. If it doesn't slow at sunset, the barometric pressure is going to change and deer will be moving about more than usual.

If the weather is stable, deer will stick to their normal routines. This is when you should pay close attention to prevailing winds, and convection and thermal currents.

## Prevailing Winds:

These are regional currents that blow in the same direction nearly every day.

(When they don't, it's usually because of changes in barometric pressure.) Such predictability makes them an important factor in choosing a stand location, especially when you're going to post in a field, bottleneck or ravine.

To determine the direction of the prevailing wind in a specific area, post there several times and keep track of where the wind comes from, and where it goes. Write down your findings! After you've done this a number of times, you'll have a good idea of the area's currents, and can then put up your stand in a spot where your scent won't be carried to where deer are likely to appear. Keep in mind that major airflow in much of the United States is from slightly southwest to slightly northeast.

## Convection Currents:

Heat rising off large objects, such as boulders, or wind deflected off trees, rocks and other terrain features, cause convection currents. They are indigenous to a particular terrain, often blow in an entirely different direction from the prevailing wind, and can cause you a lot of problems if you don't know how to read them.

While hunting whitetails in Montana a few years ago, I spied a big buck in a clear-cut at dusk. I didn't have a shot, so all I could do was watch as he moved across the open terrain. The next day I went back and chose a spot overlooking the clear-cut, with the prevailing wind blowing gently in my face. I didn't see a deer all day. The next morning I changed my location by 100 yards, and set up in a blowdown in front of a large rock ledge. Again, the wind was blowing in my face, carrying my scent away from the spot where I expected the buck to appear. After an hour, I heard the sounds of crunching brush as a deer approached. Terrific, I thought, the wind is still blowing perfectly. He'll never know I'm here.

Moments later, the buck emerged from some evergreens and moved, unconcerned, into the clear-cut. When he was about 100 yards from me, just as I was moving my rifle into position for a shot, he slammed on his brakes and, without hesitation, whirled and bounded back into the evergreens. I was dumbfounded! The wind hadn't changed direction; rather, a convection current had bounced off the ledge behind me and swirled out to the buck, who believed what his nose told him and fled immediately.

Be aware that a convection current may be present in your area, and adjust your location accordingly. To detect one, hang a strand of thread from a branch and observe how it blows in relation to the prevailing wind. At times, you'll be amazed to see it flag contrary to the direction of the prevailing wind; other times, it will conform to it.

## Thermal Currents:

Hunters should pay special attention to thermal currents in early morning and late afternoon. At dawn, as the temperature normally begins to rise, thermal currents flow upward. Conversely, as evening approaches and the temperature begins to drop, thermal currents flow downward. A hunter who takes a stand at dawn should position himself above the area where he expects to see deer. By doing so, his scent will rise. The same stand should be avoided in the evening, however, because his scent will be carried downhill.

You can beat thermal, convection and prevailing wind currents by reacting like a buck. A buck who has survived a couple of seasons has learned how to keep the prevailing winds blowing in his face, and therefore has alternate routes leading to and from bedding areas. Likewise, when you set up your stand, you should have alternate approach routes to use as wind currents dictate.

# TIPS

**Wind Tip No. 1**
*Many deer hunters don't like to go out on windy days, but such days can be good for stalking. When the wind is blowing hard, deer lie up in heavy cover and won't move. You can stalk brushy draws and other tangles and often get extremely close to the deer. This is close-in, fast shooting.*

**Wind Tip No. 2**
*For the lone hunter, still-hunting on opening day, when the woods are generally in a state of extreme flux, is a rather dubious exercise. Far better to find a place upwind of where deer normally move past in the morning, and to set up there with a ground stand or tree stand.*

**Wind Tip No. 3**
*If it's getting on toward midmorning and you've seen nary a deer, resist the urge to abandon your stand and see what you can sneak up on. On opening morning especially, if you know you've got a good stand, stay on it.*

# RATTLE

*Close-up response*

*The false rut, primary rut and post-rut periods are the best times to call in a buck.*

attling may not bring in a buck every time, but it's so effective when done correctly that every hunter should know how to do it. There are times, especially during the rut, when no other tactic can beat it.

First, the terminology. There are two basic rattling techniques: ticking (or tickling) and aggressive rattling, and each has distinct sounds and meanings. Confuse the two and you'll be wasting your hunting time. Ticking is done by lightly clicking the tips of your rattling antlers to imitate the sounds of two bucks sparring. Aggressive rattling starts with a slight ticking and builds to a crescendo of noisy, violent clashing that sounds like two bucks engaged in an all-out fight.

Ticking can be used throughout the breeding season, when bucks are just pushing each other around, not seriously fighting. Bucks that respond to ticking generally do so quite cautiously. As the rut progresses and sex-crazed bucks have zero tolerance for other males — especially transient ones that have moved into the area, searching for estrous does — more serious fights start to break out. Full-scale rattling works best now, and attracts more aggressive, bigger bucks that are generally less cautious than usual. Other times to use it are during periods of significant buck movement, intense scraping and rubbing activity, and when lone estrous does are on the move.

## When to Rattle:

There are several ideal times to rattle. Each one lasts two to three days and coincides with one of the three different rut cycles (false rut, primary rut and post-rut). From my 31 years of rattling, I have found that October 25 to 31 — what I like to call the "time of the chase" — is the prime time to draw bucks in by ticking. Bucks are starting to become belligerent and spend a lot of time chasing competitors (as well as potential estrous does) and sparring with them. Bachelor groups begin to disperse at this time, with bucks moving out of their own territory in search of receptive does.

The best time to draw in a big buck with aggressive rattling is November 10 to 13. Bucks are ranging far and wide now, and are sexually frustrated enough to be in a perpetually nasty mood. They will respond quickly and enthusiastically to the sounds of a full-scale fight during this period. Using a buck decoy can be especially effective at this time.

The final prime time for rattling is during the late rut in December usually from the 13th to the 15th. Does that have not been bred enter another estrous cycle during this phase of the rut. These does attract a lot of buck attention, as there aren't many of them to go around. Once again, bucks from surrounding areas enter the turf of resident bucks, with many skirmishes the end result.

## Time of Day:

The best time to rattle or tick is usually between 10:00 A.M. and 1:00 P.M., when the woods are quiet and generally free of hunters. Bucks often move during these off-hours, seeking does and checking and freshening scrapes. Dawn and dusk are also good times, although low-light conditions may hamper your ability to see incoming bucks, especially ones in thick cover.

## Weather:

Good rattling goes hand in hand with bad weather. A cold, overcast day with drizzling rain or spitting snow, or a forecast of precipitation, is perfect. If it has rained or snowed heavily, the following morning will also be prime. A steady breeze or wind is okay for rattling, but if there are heavy gusts, forget it, as deer are reluctant to move when they can't hear above the wind. A warm, bluebird day, when deer are apt to bed down, also means that rattling will probably be a waste of time.

## Where to Rattle:

The spot you choose to rattle from plays only a minor role. If a buck wants to respond to your rattling or ticking, he will. The important thing about location is cover. When you rattle and tick, you move a lot. You can't help it. But what you can do is break up your outline with surrounding cover. If you don't get a response to your rattling within an hour or so, consider changing locations. Some hunters believe the key to successful rattling is to be constantly on the move. These guys never stay in one spot for more than an hour unless they get a response.

Ultimately, the decision on whether to move from a spot or stay there rests with you. If you have a good feeling about it, and suspect that a buck is eventually going to show up, then it makes sense to stick around for a while. It's all a matter of timing.

# TIPS

### Rattling Tip No. 1

*Deer will often appear at a distance, then sneak in behind cover. Next thing you'll see is an antler and an eyeball peeking around a tree. To make the buck step into the open, brush the tips of your rattling antlers across one another softly just once. A soft grunt call at this point often helps persuade the buck to show itself.*

### Rattling Tips Nos. 2 & 3

*When a deer approaches, it will have its eyes zeroed in on your exact location. The best time to shoulder your gun is when the deer's head disappears behind cover. Know that the deer will try to circle downwind to catch your scent as it approaches. Be ready to shoot before it reaches your wind drift.*

Forehead glands

Nasal gland

Preorbital gland

Tarsal gland

Preputial gland

Interdigital gland

Metatarsal gland

# SCENTS

*Create hunting opportunities by making a buck's olfactory senses work for you.*

**S**avvy hunters know whitetails have external scent glands that play a significant role in their communication and behavior; different odors serve to alert, calm, attract, frighten or identify one another, even establish a deer's rank within the herd. By knowing precisely which glands the animals use, when they use them and why, you can employ the scents to elicit a variety of responses and create opportunities that wouldn't exist otherwise.

## Tarsal:

A true external gland, the tarsal is located on the inner part of the hind legs of all deer. This tan gland turns almost black as bucks urinate on it throughout the rut. Deer use tarsal gland pheromones (a type of animal chemical) several ways: as a visual and olfactory signal of a mature buck; as an alarm; as an I.D. for individual deer; and, in a mature deer in rut, as an indicator that an individual is ready to breed. When a buck is aroused, the hairs on the tarsal gland stand erect and can be seen from quite a distance by other deer. All deer urinate on the tarsal gland, contributing to its pungent odor.

To get a response during the rut, put

several drops of commercial tarsal scent on a boot pad and hang the pad from a branch near your position. The odor will permeate the area and act as a deer attractant or agitator. Don't place it on your clothing, as you don't want deer focusing on you.

## Metatarsal:

The function of the metatarsal gland, located in a white tuft of hair on the outer portion of the hind legs just above the dewclaws, is unclear. Some biologists believe it is atrophying and has no purpose. Others believe it emits a pheromone that deer use to identify and warn one another of danger. In any event, when you use metatarsal scent, use it sparingly — and be ready for anything.

## Preorbital:

This gland lies just below the inner corner of the eye, where it acts mainly as a tear duct, though deer will also rub it on bushes, branches and limbs, especially during the rut. Biologists speculate the gland secretes a pheromone that deer use to mark certain areas and to help identify one another. Hunters can achieve best results by placing a small amount of the scent on a branch directly above a mock scrape.

## Interdigital:

The offensive, potent odor of the yellow waxy substance produced by the interdigital gland is like a human fingerprint, individual to each deer. Used sparingly, interdigital scent both attracts and calms whitetails; large quantities of it, however, will do the opposite, since it signals danger. The gland is located in the cleft of the hoof, and all deer leave minute amounts of the scent as they walk. Other deer will follow a trail marked with a normal amount of it. When hunting, put only one or two drops of this commercial scent on a boot pad.

## "New" Glands:

Research has discovered additional glands that deer may use in breeding activities. According to Dr. Karl Miller, of the University of Georgia, an expert on the physiology of whitetails, three glands in particular seem to be of importance. The first, at the base of each antler, is called the forehead gland (and is sometimes referred to as the orbital gland). During the rut, the thick hairs covering the gland swell and produce a scent, specific to that buck, which he deposits on trees as he is rubbing. Other bucks and does inspecting the area will smell and lick the rubs.

The nasal gland, inside a deer's nostrils, consists of two almond-shaped sacs. Scientists speculate that bucks use this gland to mark overhead branches when making a scrape.

The preputial gland, located inside the buck's penile sheath, is still being studied. Research shows that this gland doesn't play a significant role in producing the rutting odor of bucks during the breeding season.

## Hunting Tips:

When mixing scents, especially those from glands, make sure you choose ones that don't conflict. For example, don't use a large quantity of interdigital scent with an attractant scent. Excess interdigital scent is meant to warn deer of danger, not attract them. You can, however, use just one or two drops of it with an estrous scent, as both serve to attract.

Another caution: If you use gland scents collected from recently harvested deer, use less than you would of the commercial variety, as real scent is much more potent. Gland scents, or even the urine from bladders, can be overused and lead to problems. I prefer to use commercial gland scents; most are reliable and involve much less work.

# T I P S

**Common Scents Tip No. 1**
*A simple way to make an artificial scrape is to bury a 35mm film canister containing doe-in-heat lure right at ground level. Fill the container with a piece of rolled-up cotton cloth or cotton balls to serve as a wick for liquid scent. Place a perforated cap over the container to keep dirt out and control evaporation.*

**Common Scents Tip No. 2**
*Deer urine is one of the best masking scents. It is also a good lure to use during the rut, especially when you're hunting scrapes.*

**Common Scents Tip No. 3**
*Some popular scents you won't find in sporting-goods stores include pine-scented disinfectant, pine and cedar needles, rabbit tobacco weed, apples and turpentine (as a masking scent).*

# Decoying

*By Don Oster*

*For many bowhunters, decoying is the ultimate hunting experience.*

*Silhouette decoy – the concealed hunter draws his bow and raises it up, shooting over the decoy's back.*

**R**eturning from a deer-hunting trip to his home on the edge of a small town, a friend of mine was greeted by a neighbor, who asked why he travels all over the country to hunt white-tailed deer. That morning the neighbor had watched a monster 10-pointer charge into the yard and attack my friend's life-sized bow target. If this was a fight, the deer likeness in the backyard had finished a poor second. The attacker, who must have thought he had a rival in the neighborhood, broke two legs and trashed the target's antlers.

That attack illustrates how decoys attract whitetails. In fact, whitetails approach decoys for two reasons. The first is curiosity. Deer are naturally gregarious and want to identify the stranger. The second reason occurs during the rut when bucks constantly check out does for signs of estrus.

While a doe decoy will attract bucks, a buck decoy represents a challenge during the rut. Male deer in an area know each other on sight. Except during the rut, they stay together throughout the year in bachelor groups. When a dominant buck spots a stranger in his territory, he'll be more than ready to put the trespasser in his place. If you use a buck decoy and combine it with rattling and calling – in effect setting up a mock battle between two bucks – your chances of drawing in a real one are quite good.

There are three basic types of deer decoys. Lightweight three-dimensional foam models resemble bedded deer. Rolled up and placed in a plastic bag, they are easy to carry. Hinged two-dimensional plastic decoys collapse for easy carrying, but they look realistic only when viewed from the front. Hard-plastic full-bodied decoys are bulky to carry but present the most realistic impression from all angles. On most models, antlers can be added to convert a doe to a buck. Some have adjustable ears and tail to indicate whitetail mood.

*B*arriers, such as fields, cliffs or lakes, offer another good decoy setup (below). With your back against the barrier, position the decoy in front of you, in open woods or at the edge of brush. Ideally, you should be downwind of the decoy. When a buck spots the decoy and circles downwind (blue line) to investigate it, he'll walk between you and the decoy.

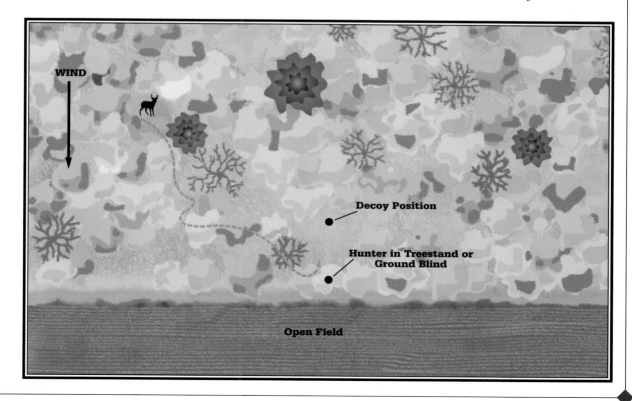

WIND

Decoy Position

Hunter in Treestand or Ground Blind

Open Field

Rattling, decoying and calling draw the attention of other hunters. A muzzle-loader hunter may safely use decoying only under special circumstances, on large tracts of private property with NO other hunters in the area. Bowhunters, even with the close-range nature of their sport, should also use caution.

## Decoying Basics:

Scent control on a decoy is a necessity. You can't make it smell exactly like a live deer, but there are some additives that can come close. First, limit human scent by spraying the decoy with scent remover. To avoid contamination, store and transport your decoy in a scent-free plastic bag and wear rubber gloves when handling it. To add deer smell, attach actual tarsal glands or drip a buck tarsal scent on the legs. Some hunters also tape small pads soaked with whitetail urine on the legs. A touch of estrous doe scent nearby may make a real buck believe the decoy is following a hot doe. Be sparing when you use scent additives; overdoing is often worse than using nothing. In the field, carry the decoy in an orange bag or cover it with a piece of fluorescent orange.

All setups must be in the open where other deer can easily see the decoy. The edges of open fields where deer regularly feed, atop a rise near a travel corridor, in a forest with minimal understory or clearings in thick cover make good sites. Bedded doe decoys are short and hard to place where they can be seen, and it may be best to pair a bedded decoy with one that is standing.

Movement can also increase a decoy's effectiveness. Some hunters tie a small, white, v-shaped cloth on the tail of a decoy so it waves gently in a breeze. They may also rig a hinged ear or tail to the decoy and move it by pulling on a fishing line stretching to their stand. Fishing line can also be used to rustle brush near the decoy, creating movement and sound to catch a buck's attention. Check state regulations before using real deer parts or mechanized moving parts on a decoy.

## Using Decoys:

Be at your setup spot before first light in the morning or well before the pre-twilight travel time in the evening. When you approach the spot and place your equipment, keep noise to a minimum. Make sure your shooting lanes are clear and you know the yardages to different points in the setup.

*Small natural openings in heavy cover are excellent places to decoy (below). Erect the decoy 20 yards from the downwind edge of the opening; then take a stand downwind and just inside the cover. Make sure you have clear shooting lanes to the decoy, as well as to the right and left (black lines), where bucks may come sneaking in along the edges of the opening (blue line). An experienced buck will be reluctant to cross the opening and is likely to pass right in front of you as he moves toward the downwind side to scent-check the decoy.*

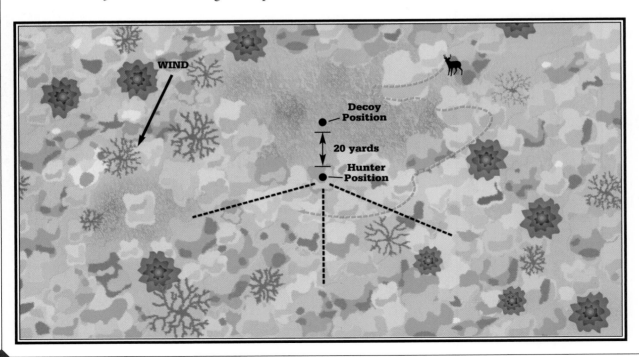

WIND

Decoy Position

20 yards

Hunter Position

Place the decoy along a buck's travel corridor, near a feeding area, or along a rub-line near his sanctuary. During the rut a buck may appear at any time of the day. Some bucks search for does around the clock. Use rattling and calling to simulate a fight. Sometimes the sight of doe and buck decoys together raises the ire of an area's buck. You want him to think a stranger is with one of his does.

Wind direction, decoy placement and stand or blind location must all be coordinated in a good setup. Once a buck has sighted the decoy, he will usually circle around and approach from the downwind side. Be in position to shoot as he circles toward the downwind side or as he moves toward the decoy. Shoot at the first good opportunity. If his attention is focused on the decoy, he may not see you draw.

Some bucks walk around the decoy to size it up. Assuming he has not smelled something fake, he may then either charge and hook the decoy or move away, depending on his size. Big antlers on a decoy can intimidate smaller bucks. The decoy's antlers should be just big enough to represent a challenge to the dominant trophy buck, which you'll shoot without hesitation.

*Rut-crazed dominant bucks will directly attack a buck decoy (above) and may try to romance a doe decoy.*

# Talk to the Animals

*By Jay Cassell*

*When to grunt and bleat and when to shut up.*

Take a look at almost any deer hunter and chances are he has a grunt call hanging around his neck. Do these devices really work, or are hunters wasting their time snorting and grunting as they make their way through the woods?

## Vocalizations:

Deer make three basic calls — the snort, the bleat and the grunt. We've all heard deer snort. You're tiptoeing through the woods, trying to get close to some heavy brush, and all of a sudden you hear a loud wheezing sound; a second later you see a white flag go bounding off through the trees. That sound is the snort, which deer make when alarmed and to alert each other to danger. For the hunter, making a snort on a deer call is of little practical use.

On the other hand, the bleat, made mostly by fawns and does, can be used to advantage. A hunter calling in an area that does frequent can usually bring in a doe by making a pleading, crying bleat. "You have to put feeling into it," says Jim Strelec of Knight & Hale Game Calls. "A lot of hunters just blow into the call and produce a dull, boring bleat. That's not going to attract any deer's attention. For a bleat call to work, you have to make it sound as if a fawn is really in distress. Cry through that call and you'll see the difference. Does will practically come running."

And following the does, one hopes, will be a buck.

## Grunt Work:

A deep, guttural vocalization made through a tube call imitates the sound bucks make when they're either with a hot doe or actively looking for one. I've seen and heard bucks grunt throughout all stages of the rut. Unfortunately, although I've used the call during that period, I've had limited success. I have come to the conclusion that with all those hunters in the woods blowing on grunt calls, many deer now associate the sound with the presence of a human being and have therefore learned to avoid it. This is true especially at the beginning of the season, when the woods are full of grunting hunters, so in the past few years I've remained quiet at this time, during the gun season in particular.

In the early bow season, or in the latter half of the gun season, I use the grunt call fairly often. And while I've spooked deer with the call — they either figured out that I was a human grunter, or else thought I was a larger buck that they didn't want to mess with — I have also called a few bucks in. It really seems to depend upon the individual buck. If a buck is hot after a doe and hears a grunt, he's more likely to investigate than if he were just going about his daily routines. Sometimes rattling antlers in conjunction with grunt calling has worked, too.

## Is Calling Worth It?:

Yes. There will be times when you spook deer with grunt calls or bleats. And there will be times when deer pay you absolutely no attention. But there will also be times when the call will either draw a buck into range or make him stop in his tracks, giving you an opportunity for a shot.

In short, calling is not a panacea but merely another tool in a deer hunter's arsenal. Don't expect too much from calls, and use them at the appropriate times.

*Grunt call*

*Bleat call*

Bowhunters often use deer calls to bring deer within shooting range (opposite).

# The *Human Scent Factor*

*By Dwight Schuh*

*Odor eliminators seem to be a hunter's dream come true. But do these products really work?*

**S**itting in a ground blind in Texas, I watched several deer pass 20 yards straight downwind from me. None ran.

In Alabama, five deer fed 80 yards straight downwind of my stand in an open field for 20 minutes. They showed no alarm. In Idaho, a whitetail buck came from my downwind side and hung around for 10 minutes under my stand, where I'd walked only minutes before. Two bears appeared downwind from my stand, played there for half an hour, and then came past my stand to the bait. They apparently never smelled me.

We all know human scent is the Achilles' heel of hunting. If only we could eliminate body odor, we could fool any big-game animal. That's why human-scent-eliminating products have exploded on the hunting market; they seem to offer a panacea for hunting's biggest headache.

But do they work? From a scientific point of view, I don't know. Without months of investigation and laboratory analyses, I have no way of knowing which products are valid, and which aren't. So I've taken them all at face value and simply tried them in the field. Frankly, the results reported above surprise me. As an innate skeptic, I figured these products were so much hype. But after two seasons, I can say that scent-elimination products, if used properly, do work. At least, I think they

*Human-scent-control products – use as part of the total odor-control system.*

can reduce body odor enough to make you a more effective hunter.

Let's distinguish "scent eliminator" from "cover scent." Scent eliminators make no attempt to mask B.O. with other, stronger aromas; they're intended to eliminate odors altogether, leaving you scent-free. Sweat itself is odorless, but bacteria attacking the fatty acids in sweat produce a gas, which is the odor you smell. Like smoke, odor has mass and can be measured, and it's cumulative, which means it builds up and produces more and more odor. Thus, the worse you smell the easier and farther animals can smell you. That's why, even if scent eliminators don't kill odor 100 percent, they're worthwhile, because they can reduce the distance at which animals will smell you.

## How De-scent Products Work:

De-scent products work in various ways. Scent Shield®, the original scent eliminator, increases the molecular weight of odor molecules, turning them from a gas into a solid. Without gas, there is no odor.

Some products, like B-Scent Free®, kill odor-causing bacteria by changing the pH to a level in which the bacteria can't live, and others kill bacteria with enzymes, like Aero-Sonics' Hunter's DeScent®. Still others, such as Atsko N-O-Dor®, oxidize bacterial wastes, leaving them odorless.

A fourth type of product absorbs odor like a sponge. Baking soda works on this principle. But most de-scent makers claim their products work better than soda. Most come as powders you sprinkle onto your clothes or store in a sealed plastic bag with your clothes to absorb odors.

## Making Them Work:

Most systems consist of a spray-on odor eliminator, laundry soap, hair and body soap, deodorant, and in some cases a scent-absorbing powder (some also include odorless oils for guns and bows).

In my experience, you must utilize the complete system or you're wasting your time and money. If you expect a few squirts from a de-scent bottle to eliminate days of accumulated B.O., forget it. On many sweaty backcountry elk and mule deer hunts, I've sprayed on gallons of scent eliminators and never seen any evidence they worked. When the wind was wrong, animals smelled me.

But, as the opening stories indicate, I've had favorable results under controlled conditions. Those conditions included a fanatical ritual. First, I washed all my clothes in de-scent soap, air dried them outside, and stored them in a plastic bag to keep out household odors. Before heading to my stand, I showered with de-scent hair and body soap and sprayed all my clothes with a de-scent spray. Also, I de-scented my bow, tree stand and daypack, and wore rubber boots sprayed with scent eliminator. Because bad breath also can alert deer, I brushed my teeth with baking soda and chewed Golden Eagle's Breath Away Gum®. Seeing deer ignore me from 20 yards downwind, I believe the ritual works.

*Scent-Loc® clothing, which features odor-absorbing, activated charcoal fused into the fabric, worn in conjunction with the odor-control system described here will also help mask your human odor.*

*Just a squirt of a de-scent product (below) isn't enough — you'll want to use the whole system.*

*Good organization is a key to conducting safe drives.*

# Late *Season* Is *Drive Time*

*By Jay Cassell*

**Last month's tactics won't work now.**

**D**eer season is on its last legs. If you haven't gotten a buck yet, you have to get serious if you want to put venison in the freezer. Tactics that worked earlier in the year won't cut it now. The rut is pretty much over, so rattling, calling or watching scrapes and rubs aren't the answers. And still-hunting heavy cover, which always gives you a chance, isn't as effective, since deer in most parts of the country are going to hear you crunching across frozen ground before you even see them.

No, if you want to get a buck, then it's time to drive. And to do that, you need planning and proper execution.

**Last Chance:**

Where I hunt, most hunters have

hung it up by the last weekend of the season. Some have already gotten a whitetail, others have simply moved on to new activities. In camp, there are often only three or four of us left, but somebody in our group usually fills his tag at the end of the season. The reason for this is that we concentrate our drives where we know deer are located.

With two to four hunters in a drive, we key in on two prime late-season areas: steep ledges, especially those on south-facing (warmer) slopes; and smaller (one- to three-acre) hemlock groves or cedar swamps.

### The Ledge Game:

When we hunt mountainside ledges, we position two standers downwind of likely deer hangouts, in spots on the slope where they can survey as far downhill or uphill as possible. The uphill stander is placed where deer will be unable to move above him, such as at the base of a rock face or an extremely steep ledge. At the agreed-upon starting time, the drivers begin walking across the ledges, with the wind at their backs, about 75 yards apart. Everyone wears hunter orange, and no one even thinks about shooting in the direction of other people. We move slowly, making minimal noise (too much commotion will spook deer into terrified flight, making any shots difficult; it's better to have deer simply get up and walk away). If any deer are kicked up, they usually move straight away from the drivers, giving the standers easy shots across the ledges; or the deer head downhill, giving the downhill stander a chance.

This type of drive also works well on ridgetops and longish saddles.

### Groves & Swamps:

When deer are holed up in hemlock groves or cedar swamps, we drive only small patches that we can effectively cover. It makes no sense to drive large hemlock groves, where deer can sneak around the drivers or simply stay hidden. We position two or three standers at the downwind perimeter of a small hemlock stand, usually where it opens up into hardwoods. Then one driver, preferably two, will enter the woods at the specified time; if there are two drivers, they move parallel to each other, never losing visual contact. Deer kicked up from the thick stuff will move either straight away from the drivers, toward the standers or out the sides in an attempt to double back. Either way, someone usually gets a shot.

Woodlots, marshes and small fields can also be effectively hunted with this type of drive.

## PLANNING

*A topo map or aerial photo of the area can help toward planning a well-coordinated drive.*

---

## I WAS ALMOST SHOT ON A DRIVE A FEW YEARS AGO:

*It was a stupid mistake, but most accidents are. I was one of three standers surrounding the perimeter of some hemlocks interspersed with blowdowns and thick brush. We were set out as a triangle, with me on the right corner. The drivers walked right by me. They didn't see me; I didn't see or hear them. Suddenly, there was a shot from just uphill of me; then a bullet came whizzing across the forest floor, kicking up leaves not 10 inches from my feet.*

*At the end of the drive, one of the drivers said he had taken a shot at a running deer but missed. When I told him that he almost shot me, he was horrified. This is a guy who has been hunting for 40 years, and it was the first time he had ever jeopardized anyone on a hunt. After that, we made a few drive rules that we follow to the letter, every year:*

- *Everyone – driver and stander – always wears hunter orange.*

- *Before the drive, we make explicit plans. Everyone knows exactly where the other people will be; and the drivers in particular always keep each other in view.*

- *No one shoots in the direction of anyone else. The only shots that can be taken will be at deer that have broken out the side of the driven area, or have gotten into an uphill or downhill position where a backstop – ledge, knoll, boulder – will stop any errant bullets. If you are unsure of your target, or of what's behind it, do not even think about shooting.*

*And a final reminder: Hunters who have already filled their tags always act as drivers since they cannot, by law, carry firearms.*

# Snow Bucks

*By Gerald Almy*

*How to hunt whitetails in winter weather — from a dusting to a blizzard.*

Snow falling through windless air, carpeting forests and fields in white, can make deer hunting magic: You move through the woods in almost total silence as the snow absorbs the thump of footfalls and the crunch of twigs and leaves underfoot. Bucks, knowing they can move quietly in a light snow, tend to travel freely, chasing does or seeking food. Scent is deadened, making it less likely deer will smell you. Sign is fresh and easy to read; tracking suddenly becomes a viable hunting method. The dark gray body of a buck stands in sharp contrast against the brilliant white background. And trailing a wounded deer is a simple task.

Yes, snow does provide some advantages. But it has a darker side, too. A densely falling snow, or thick, swirling flakes, can fog scopes and binoculars and obscure deer beyond 60 or 70 yards. In a harsh winter storm, with gusting winds and heavy accumulation, deer can bed down in thick cover and not move for days. If snow is very deep, walking any distance is difficult, which rules out still-hunting and driving. The deer themselves can't move well either, making stand-hunting unproductive. And after thawing and refreezing, old snow can crunch with each step, alerting deer to your presence.

Deep snow also affects deer diet. Where you might have pinpointed feeding activity in cropfields or oak thickets will be vacant if deer can't paw down to the ground. Instead, they'll feed on twigs and buds of young trees — locations that will require new scouting to determine how the deer are traveling.

Deer hunters must remember that snow is simply one facet of a total weather system that greatly influences deer movement and behavior. Following are the basic types of snow

*In the far north, deer yard up in a small area once deep snow makes movement difficult (opposite). Some states have regulations to protect yarded deer.*

and stages of snowstorms you might encounter, as well as the best tactics to use in each.

### Blowing Snow:

When breezes blow falling snow parallel to the ground, deer seek shelter in thick cover. Look to leeward sides of ridges, hollows and valleys.

Tactic: Still-hunt with one partner [see illustration below]. The two of you should be 50 to 125 yards apart, depending on the terrain (stay close enough to maintain occasional visual contact). One of you should be downwind of and behind the other. The leader may jump a buck and get a shot, or the deer may get up out of sight and circle downwind, giving the trailing hunter a shot. Both of you should wear fluorescent orange.

### Snow Without Wind:

Deer move more when snow falls straight down than when wind blows the flakes sideways.

Tactic: Stand-hunt along travel routes from feeding to bedding areas in the morning and evening. Situate your stand close to thick cover because bucks may be skittish. Hunt during

midday if only moderate accumulation is expected. Deer will frequently move from 10 A.M. to 2 P.M., when fewer hunters are in the woods and weather is warmest.

### Powdery Snow:

Deer are active in this type of snow, which they can easily shake off. If anything, they may move more than usual. I saw eight bucks before breaking for a midmorning breakfast when hunting in a dry-snow fall in West Virginia recently. Total accumulation was two inches. The bucks seemed to know it was just going to be a dusting that would create no difficulty in traveling.

Tactic: Since deer are moving now, stand-hunting is a good bet. If the doe-to-buck ratio is 3 to 1 or higher, lightly tick the tips of rattling antlers together for 30 to 60 seconds to pique the curiosity of nearby bucks. Also try glassing distant fields; if you see a buck, execute a stalk during the last few hours of daylight. Deer will focus on crop remains, acorns and broad-leaved weeds and grasses, since they can easily paw through light, powdery snow.

### Wet, Heavy Snow:

This type of snow, which is sometimes mixed with sleet, tends to cling to deer more, wetting their hides. Deer will typically move toward thick cover and bedding areas.

Tactic: Drive small patches of heavy cover with one or two walkers and two or three standers. Also track deer as they head toward bedding areas. Make sure you know the territory well, have a large chunk of land to hunt and use a compass.

### Shallow Snow:

Snow depth influences deer movement. Up to eight or 10 inches has little impact on a deer's ability to move freely on its normal travel routes.

*When snow is blowing, two people can increase their chances of finding a bedded buck by still-hunting near thick cover, 50 to 125 yards apart (below). The second person (B) remains downwind and a bit behind the first (A). Any buck the first hunter spooks but can't get a shot at may circle downwind to the second (red line).*

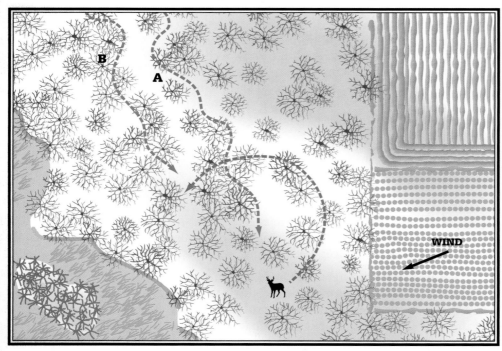

Tactic: Stand-hunt near feeding areas and clear-cuts. Also hunt midday hours. Rattle antlers if rutting activity is still present.

## Deep Snow:

In a foot or more of snow, movement becomes taxing for deer. They tend to bed in heavy cover, near feed areas where possible, and move little. Snow accumulation can vary with location; animals may gravitate to nearby spots with less snow and/or south-facing slopes where snow will melt quickly. In northern states, deer may head to yarding areas in lowland softwood swamps, where the air can be 10 to 20 degrees warmer than on exposed surrounding hills.

Tactic: Still-hunt areas with less-than-average snow accumulation, south-facing slopes, dense bedding zones, evergreen stands and swamps. Execute drives where cover is thick and where fresh sign abounds. And focus on places that have accessible woody browse such as twigs, buds and even bark.

## Crunchy Snow:

This is one of the worst conditions of all in which to hunt. It's difficult for deer to move in this type of snow and they know they make a lot of noise. Bucks therefore tend to stay bedded, or they seek out areas where the sun melts the snow enough to soften it.

Tactic: Stand-hunt overgrown fields, clear-cuts, bedding areas and south-facing slopes. Also try grunting softly. Listen carefully, since you may hear a buck walking through the snow before you see it.

## Approaching Snowstorm:

The probable intensity and duration of an approaching snowstorm should dictate your hunting strategy. If a mild system is pushing through, predicted to bring anywhere from a dusting to several inches, deer movement will seldom be curtailed. Heavy storms are another matter entirely. Often these are accompanied by a major drop in barometric pressure.

Deer seem to have built-in weather sensors. From six to 18 hours before a winter storm arrives, you'll often see whitetails feeding in areas more open and unprotected than normal for this time of year. They seem to know they can't feed or move freely once the storm arrives, and that they'll have to bed down in thick cover to conserve body heat and energy.

Tactic: This is where watching the Weather Channel pays off. Plan to be in the woods a half day to a full day before the front is scheduled to arrive and you'll see more deer movement than you would imagine possible this late in the season. Hunt from a tree stand or a ground blind near major remaining feeding areas. Grunt softly to draw deer that might be hidden in nearby cover.

## Impending Snowstorm:

As the storm nears, deer movement diminishes. Often, just before a major storm with an accompanying sharp barometric drop, virtually every animal will bed down. If it is a less intense front, deer may feed right up until the precipitation starts to accumulate, then head for cover.

Tactic: Take a stand close to bedding cover. Make a series of grunts every 20 to 30 minutes. If no deer are moving, still-hunt or put on drives in thick bedding cover or yarding areas.

## During a Snowstorm:

Once a bad snowstorm begins, deer will be bedded in dense cover: honeysuckle groves, thick sapling growths, greenbriars, laurel, swamps, riverbottoms, brushy draws, benches just below mountain crests and conifer thickets. No animals will be in fields or open woods at this time.

Tactic: With deer concentrated in thick cover, still-hunting is a good method. Also execute small drives, covering specific patches of thick cover. Watch the intensity of the storm and call it quits before you endanger yourself or your partners.

## After a Snowstorm:

When the storm passes, the barometer rises, skies clear and deer begin moving almost immediately. Ideally the high-pressure system will clear out the storm just before dawn, so the burst of activity will come right as you begin hunting. If the storm ends at sunset, deer may move a lot at night, unless the weather is bitterly cold. This will cut down the intensity of their movement somewhat, but there will still be above-average deer activity and most of it will be concentrated around feeding areas.

Tactic: Be in position at dawn, or head out immediately if a storm breaks during the day. Stand-hunt near farmland with crop residues; wheat, oat and rye fields; and woods with remaining acorns. If snow is deep, switch to areas with grapes, woody browse and other late foods. Click antlers lightly or grunt to entice nearby bucks. Use restraint if you see smaller deer, because this is one time you may get a shot at a truly huge buck.

# *Deer Hunting's Terrible* 10
## *(Problems, That Is)*

### By Gerald Almy

*When you have mishaps afield, what you need is a sense of humor.*

## Where Are All the Deer?:

**1** Seeing little deer activity during the day, but sign is prevalent. This is a problem I often had to deal with during my early years of deer hunting. There would be tracks, droppings, well-used trails, even beds. But when I placed my stands nearby, I saw no deer.

It finally became clear I was hunting areas that were used almost exclusively at night. Hunting pressure was heavy enough that bucks and even does were vacating those open areas and moving into denser cover before first shooting light.

By following trails and sign back into thickets, I began seeing animals. Usually I encountered does just a short distance into the brush and thicker timber. But when I worked even farther back into swamps, grown-over clear-cuts and rugged sections of surrounding mountains, more and bigger bucks showed themselves.

There aren't always well-marked runways to these areas. Sometimes the trail from the night-feeding area will peter off, particularly where an older buck takes different routes to his daytime bedding areas. At this point it's time to use your topo map and do some serious footwork to find areas where heavy cover or steep terrain would likely attract a buck. Then it's a matter of putting up a stand nearby and watching early and late in the day.

## Controlling the Crowds:

**2** Other hunters moving through the woods near your stand. This is a common problem, particularly in hard-hunted Eastern states. If you've done lots of pre-season scouting, patterned the animals in your hunting area, and pinpointed natural deer movements that should yield a buck, it's disheartening to have a hunter come ambling through at 9:00 A.M. because he got cold.

There are two solutions to this. One is to give up on areas where many hunters are likely to be encountered — in short, places close to roads. Instead, hike in at least a mile, set up camp before the season, and chances are you'll never see another hunter.

The other solution is to use hunters to your advantage. On your map plot the locations of parking lots or wide spots in the road so you'll know where most hunters will enter. Look for rough terrain, swamps or areas of thick vegetation nearby, sneak into them well before first light, and take a stand.

By getting a jump on other hunters, you'll already be waiting at escape areas when deer flee the pressure at first light. Circle wide around terrain where you think deer might be before first light, making sure your stand is positioned downwind of the routes they'll use when they head to the escape areas.

**S**uccessful deer hunting comes down to problem solving. Each time we enter the woods, there are new challenges and new mysteries of animal behavior to unravel. How much we become a part of the natural world, how well we take up the role of the predator — these factors determine how successful we are in solving whatever problems we encounter. Some, however, are much tougher than others.

### Too Few Trophy Deer:

Seeing a few small bucks, but no large racks. This is a common complaint from hunters. It's not surprising, since in most states the majority of bucks harvested are 1½-year-olds that have just become legal. Until more hunters pass up such bucks, small deer are what they'll see most often, since trophy potential isn't reached until four to seven years of age.

By carefully choosing where you hunt, however, you *can* up the odds of seeing larger bucks. One choice is a private, managed hunting property where only a small number of mature bucks are taken each year.

There are other options, though. When restocking efforts are under way in areas of marginal habitat or low populations, hunting may be closed down for several years. Once seasons are reopened, there's often a large percentage of older bucks available. Wildlife refuges are also opened periodically when deer become too numerous and managers need to thin the herd.

Limited-permit areas are another good bet. When only a small number of hunters are allowed into an area, chances of more older deer being present are much better. Finally, don't overlook public areas that are hard to penetrate by the average hunter. Remote wilderness areas without easy access often hold a surprising number of bucks with above-average racks because other hunters don't make the extra effort to seek them out.

### Walk the Walk, Talk the Talk:

Not being able to last all day on stand. To last successfully for 10 hours or more on watch, you need to start with a certain level of comfort. Bring enough clothing to stay warm while sitting immobile for extended periods. Don't wear them all as you walk in. Instead, dress lightly and carry the rest tied to your pack. Get to your stand, cool down from the hike, *then* slowly put the extra clothes on. Wear underwear of a wicking material such as Thermax® or polypropylene, topped with several layers of wool or synthetics. Don't forget gloves and headgear that covers the ears.

Besides sufficient clothing, pack plenty of juice or water and food. Finally, bring a plastic jug with a top to use as a urinal.

Staying on stand all day also requires the right attitude. Don't look at it as an endurance contest. You need not remain 100 percent immobile. You can slowly turn your head to look at the woods in all directions around you. In fact, it's important to do that so you don't miss possible deer movement. I also like to sit for a period, then stand every now and then after checking carefully to see if any deer are present before I get up.

There are times when it's best *not* to stay put all day. If the weather is hot, hunting pressure is low, and the rut is not on, for instance, chances of seeing a buck at midday are slim. You might do better to rest back at camp. But during most modern firearms seasons, the rut is on and many hunters are in the woods, making it worthwhile to stay put. If you have chosen the stand location carefully, you'll have confidence that at any minute a buck could show itself. That knowledge makes it easier to last a full day — or at least a large part of it — on stand.

### What to Do on Girls' Night Out:

When you are seeing more does than bucks. Several explanations for this problem are possible. In many areas, particularly where the deer population is high, the sex ratio of the herd is badly out of balance, and it's not unexpected to see mostly does. These are usually areas with huge herds, and the best bet is to work through the does until you find a legal buck among them. If the rut is on, eventually one will show.

Of course, if you don't enjoy hunting areas with such an out-of-kilter sex ratio, there are solutions. Contact your state game and fish department and find out from wildlife biologists where the herd composition is more balanced. Seek out these areas and you may not see as many deer, but chances are every third or fourth animal will be a buck. Odds are, too, that it will have a larger rack than those in the heavily unbalanced areas.

Another possible reason for seeing more does than bucks is that you're hunting areas where the terrain is too "soft" and accessible. After the first bit of hunting pressure, larger bucks head for rough, hard-to-penetrate terrain, leaving does in fields and open woods. Seek these hideouts and you'll likely find the bucks.

### How to Go the Distance:

Seeing deer too far away to shoot. The typical shot at a whitetail is at about 50 yards. Because of this — and tradition — many hunters arm themselves with "brush guns" such as the 30-30 or 35 Remington.

There's nothing wrong with these calibers. But there are others that will do just as well in the woods and brush and *also* allow you to shoot that occasional buck you see 200 yards across a canyon or at the edge of a 250-yard-long soybean field.

Opt for a flatter-shooting rifle such as a 270, 280 or 30-06. Then, with practice, you can take deer out to 250 yards, even 300, if you feel comfortable with that distance.

### 7 I Can See Clearly Now:

Sighting deer at dusk and dawn, but not clearly enough to shoot. This is a problem that plagues many hunters. It can be extremely frustrating to do everything right and then see deer in light that's too dim either to identify the size of a rack or to see precisely enough for a clean shot.

With iron sights you lose the best hour of the day's hunting — 30 minutes at first light and 30 more in the evening. Invest in a quality scope and you'll up your hunting success dramatically. Inexpensive, cheaply made scopes will handicap you and deprive you of clear, well-illuminated viewing during those first and final minutes of daylight, when the biggest bucks often fleetingly cross our paths.

Invest in a quality scope and you'll never regret a penny you spent on it. A fixed-power 4x will do, but most hunters will be happier with a good variable in the 2-7x, 3-9x or 1.5-6x range. These provide the option of opening the field of view for close hunting in tight cover and cranking up the magnification on long shots. In addition to the scope, invest in a good pair of binoculars, minimum 8 power or, better still, 9 or 10.

### 8 In a Rut, Out in the Cold:

Post-rut, cold-weather bucks. After the rut and weeks of intense hunting pressure, finding an antlered deer can be a real challenge. Food and comfort become important concerns for deer at this time, as does escape from hunting pressure. These three factors are your keys to finding

post-rut bucks. Look for out-of-the-way food supplies, such as honeysuckle or a secluded wheat or clover field near a thicket, and areas with fresh tracks nearby, then hunt very early and late from a downwind stand.

If the weather is unusually bitter, look for south-facing slopes on mountains and areas protected from strong breezes. Finally, look for dense escape cover. This should be as thick as a jungle, high on slopes or far from roads, where most hunters don't venture. A rough, craggy ridge, dense swamp, grown-up cutover far from parking areas — these are the secret spots whitetails head to after the rut is over, seeking sanctuary until the season ends.

### 9 The Wind They Call Mariah:

Coping with extremely windy weather. Strong wind is not conducive to good hunting. It makes bucks skittish and overly alert. The solution is to find areas that aren't windswept. Look for spots in dense swamps or thick conifer groves where the wind doesn't penetrate.

Another tactic that works is to head for the lee side of mountains and hills, where the terrain blocks the brunt of the breezes. Whitetails will often head for these areas, and you can either still-hunt for them there or take a stand where sign is abundant and a good supply of food such as acorns is available.

### 10 A Hot Time in the Woods:

Unusually hot weather. This is one of the toughest challenges you will face when hunting for white-tails. When temperatures reach the 60s and 70s, daytime whitetail movement is minimal. Deer tend to travel at night in these conditions, and the best course of action is to hunt as close to darkness as possible, meaning the crack of dawn and the last hour of dusk, when cool weather begins to claim the land again.

I've also had some success in hot weather by hunting dense, shady areas, particularly near springs and creeks, where the deer go to escape the heat and get a drink. Another good place to check is high on ridges, where fresh breezes blow, lowering the temperature a few degrees.

# MAKING THE SHOT

**S**uddenly, there he is! You didn't see him coming; rather, he just materialized from out of nowhere, standing still, close enough for you to see the vapor coming from his nostrils. You've dreamed of this moment, thought about it and planned for it – and now it's here (the moment of truth).

All the work of scouting, studying, patterning, practice shooting, picking ambush spots, setting up blinds has finally paid off, putting this opportunity at hand. How will you handle it? Campfire stories abound of hunters doing all the wrong things in the presence of a big buck. Will you be able to perform, or will you be just another sorry tale?

It seems simple to place a projectile from your weapon into the vitals – that paper-plate-sized target you've practice-shot successfully so many times. It doesn't matter whether you are bow-hunting from a tree stand or shooting across a canyon with a flat-shooting rifle, your preparation and practice should now pay off.

The adrenaline rush is on; sweaty palms, shaky hands, stomach going into knots – no way to prepare for this stuff. Surely he can hear your pounding heart. If you didn't get this worked up, you probably wouldn't be here, because it just wouldn't be worth all the effort. Through all the nerves, somehow, the weapon comes up, the hands are steady, the aim is true and the deed is done. You made the shot.

*– Don Oster*

*This should be a sure shot at such close range (left). Most deer in the United States are shot at distances of less than 100 yards.*

# The Point of Aim

*By Tom Gresham*

*How to hit the vital areas from any angle.*

The deer hunter watched his guide inch forward on hands and knees, looking for another drop of blood.

"I don't understand it," said the hunter. "I held behind the shoulder." They had been tracking the buck for almost an hour; it would be another 30 minutes before they found him. The bullet had, indeed, struck behind the shoulder – five inches behind. But because the buck had been angled toward the hunter, the bullet had passed *behind* the lungs – a gut shot that left the guide shaking his head and the hunter wondering what had gone wrong.

The traditional hunting theory, that you should always aim behind the shoulder, had betrayed yet another hunter. On paper, the concept seems infallible: Place your bullet or slug just back of the shoulder to hit the lungs. In reality, your chances of actually getting an unimpeded broadside shot at the heart/lung area are small. You are more likely to see a buck walking toward or away from you, either directly or at an angle.

The key to dropping a buck with the first shot is to think in three dimensions. You aren't trying to hit the side of a deer; you're trying to put your bullet or slug into the heart or lungs. If you imagine these vital organs as sitting squarely between the shoulders, with the heart quite low, you can then picture the correct angle no matter how the buck is positioned.

Some hunters favor the neck shot, but I've never liked it. A whitetail's neck is small, and if you miss the spine, there's a good chance of a crippling wound. Sure, some neck shots can produce spectacular kills, as will any hit in the central nervous system. But neck shots also result in a lot of misses. I prefer an aiming point that allows me to be less than perfect and still get my buck.

Study the aiming angles presented on these pages. Memorize them, then think them through before going hunting. When that buck steps out, you may have only seconds to shoot. If you know your aiming point for every angle, you'll automatically put the crosshairs on the right spot.

If you have a broadside shot and are using a rifle in a good deer caliber or a shotgun loaded with slugs, aim at the shoulder. Yes, you will ruin a little meat, but you'll get your buck. As an aiming point, the shoulder affords a wide margin of error: A shot that goes slightly high hits the spine; slightly low, and it hits the heart. Too far back catches the lungs, and too far forward still has a good chance of making a neck shot. A hit right on the shoulder breaks bones and destroys the lungs. Most deer will drop on the spot, and the few that run rarely get far.

## HEAD-ON SHOT

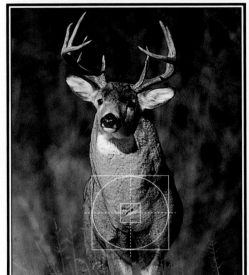

A angles other than broadside, you have to think 3-D. Aim for the vital area within the buck's chest.

If he is facing you directly, put the crosshairs squarely on his brisket.

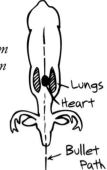

### LET THEM PASS

*Many bowhunters prefer to let the deer pass beneath their tree stand and take the shot from a downward, rear angle. This allows the archer to draw without the deer seeing movement.*

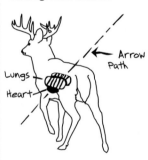

## FORWARD-ANGLE SHOT

W hen he angles toward you, the aiming point shifts closer to the point of the shoulder, but the important thing is to be aiming at the lungs.

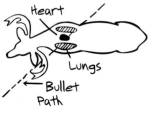

## ANGLING-AWAY SHOT

W hen the buck is angling away from you, aim as if you want the bullet to hit the shoulder on the opposite side.

If you are in a tree stand and the buck is directly below you, aim – again, keep the angles in mind – at the heart/lung area. Chances are you'll break the spine as well as hit the vital organs. A straight going-away shot is risky, and should be avoided if possible.

Not all shots are horizontal, and those vertical angles can cause problems. In the steep slopes along Idaho's Salmon River, I twice missed a mule deer buck when I tried to hold high for a long-range shot. It was below me at an acute angle, walking up a slope on the far ridge. Finally, I held right on him and put the 175-grain Hornady bullet from my 7mm Rem Mag squarely between the shoulder blades. Its spine severed, the mule dropped immediately.

## ABOVE OR BELOW SHOT

**Hunter**

**Actual distance: 350 Yds.**

**Target**

**Horizontal distance: 250 Yds.**

Shots taken at extreme angles — both up and down — tend to go high. The trajectory is affected by the horizontal distance to the target, not the actual distance. So if the deer is 350 yards away, but at an extreme angle up or down, the bullet will hit above – not below – the line of sight, because the horizontal distance is only 175 yards. On shots at extreme angles, either up or down, aim one-third of the way up from the buck's belly line.

## LONG SHOT

Big-game guides agree that hunters miss 10 bucks by shooting high for every one they miss by shooting low. When hunters unfamiliar with the distances of the West head into the big country, they tend to overestimate the ranges. Sure, 300 yards is a long shot, especially when you're used to seeing deer at 80, but a flat-shooting rifle sighted in properly doesn't need your help. A 30-06 with a 150-grain bullet, sighted in three inches high at 100 yards, drops only four inches below the line of sight at 300 yards. At 250 yards, it is right on. Each year untold numbers of hunters take that 250-yard shot, hold "just over his back," then shoot just over his back.

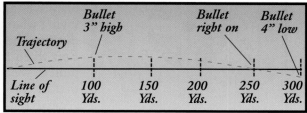

| | **Bullet 3" high** | | **Bullet right on** | **Bullet 4" low** |
|---|---|---|---|---|
| **Trajectory** | | | | |
| **Line of sight** | 100 Yds. | 150 Yds. | 200 Yds. | 250 Yds. | 300 Yds. |

Carve this into your rifle's stock: For the first shot, shoot at hair. Even if you have overestimated the range, the bullet can still drop a foot before you miss.

# The Quest for Accuracy

*By Grits Gresham*

*T est your rifle's capability at the range. Use sandbags for a solid setup. Do not let anything touch the barrel. Be patient; let the barrel cool between shots.*

"**M**y rifle just won't shoot!" That all-too-familiar lament is repeated a few thousand times each year, from coast to coast and border to border. It's muttered under the breath at shooting ranges. Deer camps resound with the tune. It's wafted over the counter at gun stores, sometimes by hunters holding a brand-new rifle. It reaches every gun maker in the nation, by letter, by phone, and now by fax.

The shooters singing that plaintive tune aren't really saying what they mean. It's not that the rifle won't go *bang* when the trigger is pulled. What they mean is that the rifle won't shoot accurately.

Ah, accuracy. The quest for ultimate accuracy began long ago and will never end. Although some smoothbores delivered

fairly decent results, the ball or bullet leaving them couldn't escape a knuckle-balling tendency. Rifling, which spins the bullet and stabilizes its flight, was the giant step.

Many of us wrongly think, however, that tight groups are a modern phenomenon. Consider a group fired in June of 1858: 50 shots into about 2.16 inches at 220 yards, which translates into minute-of-angle performance.

## The Benchrest Effect:

That great group fired 135 years ago was a benchrest group. Then, as today, accuracy buffs of the benchrest persuasion strove to discover the smallest details of rifle and ammunition construction, sighting equipment and shooting techniques that would shrink groups toward the ultimate one-holer. We're just about at that point.

Modern scoring methods measure groups from the centers of the two holes farthest away from each other. The ultimate group, therefore, would

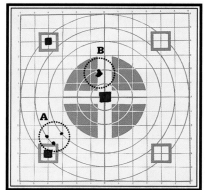

*Today's factory ammo enables most hunters to shoot 1-inch groups at 100 yards (A). For the hunter desiring maximum accuracy, handloaded ammo can produce the tightest shot groups (B).*

## LOAD – NO LOAD

*No, this isn't about mutual funds. It's about the probable minority of big-game hunters who want to coax just a little more accuracy out of their ordinary rifles than they find in factory loads. Possibly beset with "fiddlitis," these people are willing to buy and test many different powders, loads and bullets to find that sweet spot for their rifle. Is a $1/2$-inch group necessary? In most hunting situations – no. So what do these attempts at triple nail driving really produce? Well, very good accuracy and a knowledge of their bullet's trajectory when needed. But the main thing is confidence in the equipment and shooting ability. Given some allowances for field conditions and a bit of pilot error, these folks know they can make the shot.*

be .000-inch. Twenty years ago the world record for five shots at 100 yards was .070-inch. It's much better than that today, but just trying to measure .070-inch on a ruler shows why further improvement is so challenging.

The achievements of benchrest experimenters over the past decades have had an enormous impact far beyond their own ranks. From them, hunters learned what *could* be accomplished, and rifle manufacturers were encouraged (badgered, pushed) to improve the accuracy of their factory offerings.

A rifle, however, is only as accurate as the ammunition being fired in it, which made it necessary that ammo improve along with the rifles. Provided that the bullets being used are good ones, the most important accuracy aspect of a round is that its muzzle velocity be consistent from shot to shot. It will vary, but ammo manufacturers strive for the smallest variation possible. So have bench-resters, forever, with

their handloaded rounds. And so, now, do the tens of thousands of varmint shooters and big-game hunters who load their own.

Factory ammunition is now measurably more accurate than it has ever been. For some of it, only the most efficient and dedicated handloader can conjure up further improvement.

*Although prone may be the most solid field-shooting position, sitting is next best and will be the one you'll likely be able to use in actual field conditions. Using a quick-sling wrap will aid aiming stability.*

# EQUIPMENT

◆

**E**ver wonder why so many deer hunters own pick-up trucks or large recreational vehicles? The answer is simple: They need to carry their gear. A totally equipped hunter who wants to take advantage of the full-menu offering of regular and special deer seasons and uses several different hunting techniques can accumulate enough equipment to fill a good-sized truck.

Basic clothing — camo (you can never have too much), underwear, socks, gloves, boots and hats for hunting in both warm and cold conditions — can make quite a pile. A weapon or weapons, allowing hunting in special seasons, can include rifle, handgun, shotgun, bow or muzzleloader, with, of course, the appropriate sights and ammunition or projectile for each. Other needed equipment, such as binoculars, knives, ropes and an orange vest, can set up a hunter for sneak or still hunting on the ground.

Want to glass and stalk? Add a spotting scope. Climb a tree? Add stands (as with camo, hard to have too many), then add something to aid the ascent up the tree and pruning shears or a saw to clear shooting lanes. Decoying, rattling and calling necessitate decoys, rattling antlers and grunt and bleat calls. You don't smell good to a deer, so add a box containing both scent eliminators and cover-up scents. Add another box of attractants for use during the rut.

Other equipment can include a daypack or packboard, a rangefinder and GPS unit. This completes the truck or vehicle load. All this stuff won't be necessary for any one outing in the woods. However, it's nice to know that any forgotten item is nearby. Always carry the GPS; you may need it to find your way back to the truck.

*— Don Oster*

# Easy-Shooting Rifles

*By Clair Rees*

**Firearms and cartridges that do the job on deer, without punishing the hunter.**

**R**ecoil doesn't bother you? Try this experiment next time you're at the shooting range. Turn your back while a friend loads the magazine of your deer rifle with anywhere from one to four cartridges – his choice. When he hands the rifle back, you won't know how many rounds it contains.

Now aim and shoot repeatedly at a bull's-eye 50 yards away. Your friend, wearing effective hearing protection, should stand safely to one side (well back from the muzzle) and observe. If you don't close your eyes, grimace, jerk the trigger or flinch even slightly when the rifle unexpectedly goes click instead of BOOM,

*G*uns with less recoil can help a new hunter start out correctly.

recoil truly doesn't bother you. And I'd like to meet you and shake your hand — you're a rare breed.

Every shooter is affected by recoil. Some learn to manage it and shoot powerful hunting rifles accurately; others do not. Practice helps, but doesn't always provide a cure for flinching. Even experienced sportsmen flub shots on occasion, and recoil is often a contributing factor. Magnums aren't the only offenders, either. The jarring thump of a 270 or 30-06 is enough to make many riflemen miss their mark. In fact, we'd all shoot better if our rifles didn't kick so hard.

Your deer rifle doesn't have to thump you, though. You can reduce recoil by selecting the right cartridge, using a heavier rifle, or adding a muzzle brake. The action you choose can even make a difference. An eight-pound rifle shoots softer than a six-pound ultralight model. An autoloader delivers less apparent recoil than a bolt-action, single-shot or lever-action rifle.

## Light but Deadly Loads:

Cartridge choice is important. A seven-pound 30-06 shooting the popular 150-grain factory load kicks twice as hard as a 257 Roberts shooting a 117-grain bullet. Not surprisingly, most shooters are capable of better marksmanship with the softer-kicking rounds.

There are trade-offs, however. When you opt for a light-recoiling cartridge, you get less punch at both ends. In the deer woods, this often translates into marginal killing performance at extended range. For instance, a 165-grain bullet fired from a 30-06 strikes with 2350 foot-pounds of energy at 100 yards, and still has 1220 foot-pounds remaining at the 400-yard mark. In contrast, a 100-grain bullet from a 243 Winchester factory load delivers 1516 foot-pounds at 100 yards and just 882 foot-pounds at 400 yards.

To be effective on whitetails and mulies, a rifle bullet needs to strike with at least 1000 foot-pounds of energy. That makes the 30-06 a solid performer out to the 400-yard mark, while the 243 pretty much poops out past the 300-yard mark. But since most deer are shot at ranges well shy of 200 yards — with many of those less that 100 yards away — recoil-sensitive hunters find this trade-off well worthwhile.

## Weight: The Great Tamer:

If you hunt deer in mountain or desert country, or simply aren't willing to pass up those occasional long shots, there are ways to ease the bite of even a hard-kicking magnum. One proven way to reduce the punishment any

## STARTING OUT

*Start a novice shooter out with a 22 shooting at short-range targets. Help the beginner learn gun safety, good habits such as how to sight, squeeze the trigger and shoot accurately in a relaxed, nonthreatening atmosphere. Plinking at targets is a fun way to get a person started shooting. Following smallbore practice, carefully move the beginner up to a centerfire to learn shooting at longer distances.*

*A common mistake a well-meaning parent, spouse or friend can make is to introduce a novice shooter, regardless of sex or age, to a hard-kicking rifle on their first outing. To one who is new to the game, managing sights and sandbags, squeezing the trigger, then withstanding the roar and stomp of a centerfire can be ultraintimidating. In only a few shots, the beginner may develop an uncorrectible shooter's flinch that could last a lifetime. The experience might also cause a newcomer to forget the whole idea altogether, cheating him or her out of a lifetime of shooting and hunting fun.*

cartridge doles out is to use a heavier rifle. Pass up those featherweight models in favor of something heftier.

A Ruger Model 77 Ultra Light model in 270 Winchester weighs only six pounds, while Ruger's M77 Express rifle is a full pound-and-a-half heavier. Weatherby's Vanguard rifle scales eight pounds, while Browning's Model 1885 single shot runs just four ounces shy of the nine-pound mark. The right scope, mount and sling can add another pound or so.

The extra weight reduces recoil. A 270 firing a 130-grain factory load recoils with 22.7 foot-pounds of force in a seven-pound rifle. The same load generates 18.7 foot-pounds in an 8½-pound rifle, and just 15.9 foot-pounds in a 10-pound firearm. The 10-pound 270 kicks only 1.7 foot-pounds harder than a seven-pound 6mm Remington rifle — and few consider the 6mm punishing to shoot.

If you're supersensitive to recoil, you can tame kick even further with a bull-barreled varmint rifle. Remington, Ruger and Savage all offer nine- or 10-pound varmint rifles, while Winchester's "Heavy Varmint" Model 70 scales a hefty 10¾ pounds. These rifles sport 24- or 26-inch barrels and are more tiring to tote than is an ultralight carbine, but they sure soften recoil. Scoping a Model 70 varmint rifle can bring the weight to an even 12 pounds; in 243 Winchester chambering, recoil will be held to a powder-puff seven foot-pounds.

## The Automatic Advantage:

Yet another way to tame the punishment hunting cartridges dole out is to carry an autoloader. The cycling of the self-loading action uses up a small amount of recoil energy, but the real benefit comes in how the remaining energy is meted out to your shoulder. A bolt-action, or any other fixed-breech rifle, delivers a short, sharp blow. Autoloaders spread that recoil out over several milliseconds — more like a firm push than a rabbit punch. The energy transmitted to your shoulder may be the same, but the autoloader is a lot more pleasant to shoot. Recoil pads work in much the same way — they spread recoil out over a longer time span, as well as over a larger surface area.

Remington's Model 7400 autoloader and Browning's BAR both weigh around 7½ pounds in most deer calibers. The Browning is also offered in four magnum chamberings; the magnums scale 8 pounds 6 ounces before you add a scope.

## Accessories to Duck the Punch:

The single most effective way to reduce your rifle's recoil requires a little gunsmithing. It'll cost you somewhere in the neighborhood of $200 to have a muzzle brake installed, but these devices work surprisingly well. Good muzzle brakes can actually reduce recoil 50 to 70 percent. They're most efficient with high-velocity rounds: The faster the bullet, the better the brake works.

A muzzle brake consists of a screw-on tube, or muzzle extension, with a number of holes drilled in it. The holes can be drilled into existing barrel muzzles on some rifles as well. These holes divert expanding gases sideways and to the rear. This goes a long way toward off-setting recoil forces. There are trade-offs, however. In addition to being relatively costly, muzzle brakes can be extremely hard on your ears. Actual noise level rises only 10 to 15 decibels (an increase of less than 20 percent), but the report is much sharper and more piercing. Hearing protection is definitely recommended.

There are several excellent muzzle brakes on the market, including the KDF Recoil Arrestor, Barnes Straightline Quiet Brake, Gentry Quiet Brake and the New Answer System brake. The Mag-Na-Port system also tames recoil, but is better known for reducing muzzle jump. Ask your local gunsmith for details or write directly to the manufacturer.

What's your best bet for a low-recoiling deer rifle? If you're willing to limit your shots to 125 yards or so, Ruger's Mini Thirty autoloader is the least punishing deer rifle on the market. With iron sights, the rifle produces just 6.2 foot-pounds of recoil. Add a scope, and it kicks with less than 5½ foot-pounds of force. Because it's an autoloader, felt recoil is even less. In an 8½-pound rifle, the 257 Roberts cartridge develops 8.8 foot-pounds of recoil. The 243 Winchester packs a 9.8 foot-pound kick. Both are effective out to 300 yards. If you find that much recoil a bit bothersome, adding a good muzzle brake will more than halve that punch. Cartridges like the 6mm Remington and 7x57mm Mauser are also noted for their civilized shooting manners, and are great choices for hunting deer.

The absolute ultimate in a light-kicking 300-yard deer rifle? Probably a 243 Browning or Remington autoloader fitted with a muzzle brake and a one-pound scope. This kind of rig should practically pull you *forward* when you shoot.

# RECOIL COMPARISON CHART

| Cartridge | Bullet Weight grains | Muzzle Velocity feet per second | Rifle Weight pounds | Recoil foot-pounds |
|---|---|---|---|---|
| 7.62x39mm | 123 | 2300 | 7 | 6.2 |
| | | | 8.5 | 5.1 |
| | | | 10 | 4.3 |
| 250 Sav | 100 | 2820 | 7 | 9.4 |
| | | | 8.5 | 8.5 |
| | | | 10 | 6.6 |
| 30-30 Win | 170 | 200 | 7 | 10.4 |
| 44 mag | 240 | 1760 | 7 | 10.6 |
| 257 Roberts | 117 | 2650 | 7 | 10.7 |
| | | | 8.5 | 8.8 |
| | | | 10 | 7.5 |
| 243 Win | 100 | 2960 | 7 | 11.9 |
| | | | 8.5 | 9.8 |
| | | | 10 | 8.4 |
| 6mm Rem | 100 | 3100 | 7 | 14.2 |
| | | | 8.5 | 11.7 |
| | | | 10 | 9.9 |
| 7x57mm | 140 | 2650 | 7 | 15.3 |
| | | | 8.5 | 12.6 |
| | | | 10 | 10.7 |
| 7mm - 08 Rem | 140 | 2860 | 7 | 18.3 |
| | | | 8.5 | 15.1 |
| | | | 10 | 12.8 |
| 308 Win | 150 | 2820 | 7 | 19.2 |
| | | | 8.5 | 15.8 |
| | | | 10 | 13.4 |
| 30-06 | 150 | 2910 | 7 | 21.6 |
| | | | 8.5 | 17.8 |
| | | | 10 | 15.1 |
| 270 Win | 130 | 3060 | 7 | 22.7 |
| | | | 8.5 | 18.7 |
| | | | 10 | 15.9 |
| 7mm Rem Mag | 140 | 3175 | 7 | 28.2 |
| | | | 8.5 | 23.2 |
| | | | 10 | 19.7 |
| 300 Win Mag | 150 | 3290 | 7 | 36.4 |
| | | | 8.5 | 30.0 |
| | | | 10 | 25.5 |

Recoil scale: 0  5  10  15  20  25  30  35  40

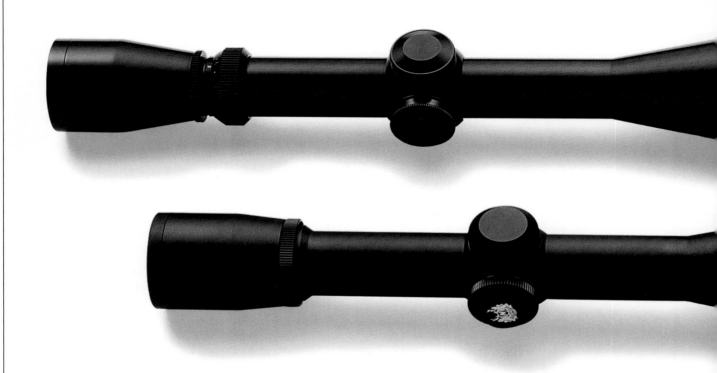

# How *Scopes* Help You Hit

*By Wayne van Zwoll*

*The best rifle in the world won't improve your shooting unless you know what your scope can and cannot do.*

**R**ifles that aren't drilled for scopes are about as common now as apartments without phone jacks. No wonder! A rifle scope makes your target bigger and brighter. It speeds aiming because the reticle appears in the same plane as the target. The modern hunting scope is fogproof, durable and compact. Scopes are even displacing iron sights on handguns, shotguns and muzzleloaders.

But scopes haven't always held the edge. Those used by Civil War snipers were as long as rifle barrels and as dim as Grandma's view of Scotch. Hunters had no use for their fragile mounts and reticles, their bulky adjustments or their great weight.

Obviously, hunting scopes have come a long, long way since then. But not every modern scope is perfect. Scopes can be made cheaper in as many ways as they can be built better. Quality scopes are still the best bargains.

### Pluses and Minuses of Magnification:

For a long time the 4X has been touted as the best all-around scope power for big-game hunters. Truly, if you were stuck with a 3X or 6X for the rest of your life, you'd find it adequate. But

antlers. Bad logic. Most variables for big-game guns have a top end of 6 to 10 power, about the magnification you get in binoculars. Binoculars are easier to use and more effective. Besides, using a scope to search for game is dangerous. You could find a hunter behind that crosswire!

Field of view, or the size of an area visible through a scope, is the obvious sacrifice when you boost power, because the bigger the target image, the smaller the field. A typical 4X scope might offer a field of view of 38 feet at 100 yards. An 8X scope gives you only half that field. Finding a buck walking through brush 100 yards away, in a field of view of 19 feet, isn't always a simple task. The only way to increase field of view would be to increase the size of the ocular lens — but then your bolt handle wouldn't clear it.

High magnification brings other woes. Eye relief (the range of distance between your eye and the ocular lens that gives you a full target picture) is most generous on low-power scopes. High-power scopes have "critical" eye relief: The sight picture blacks out if your eye is just a bit too far forward or back. For urgent shooting, critical eye relief is as useful as a fork in soup.

## How Bright?:

The objective lens doesn't have anything to do with field of view or eye relief. It does affect light transmission. Objective lens diameter (mm) divided by magnification yields "exit pupil," a measure of light transmission. Our eyes have pupils that dilate in the dark to about 7.1mm and constrict in daylight to 2.5. Maximum dilation during normal hunting hours is around 6, even on a cloudy evening. A scope with an exit pupil of 6 gives you all the light your eyes can use (assuming top-quality multicoated lenses). A 4X scope with 32mm objective has a large exit pupil of 8. A 6x32 scope's exit pupil is 5.3, on the small side for woods hunting. My 6x42 Leupold has an exit pupil of 7, with an objective bell that still lets me use low rings. I'm not sold on variable scopes with 50mm objectives. They're bulky

*S copes are available in two types — variable power (top), which allow you to change magnification, and fixed power (bottom).*

a 4X has the best mix of field, brightness and magnification.

Hunters who like variables reject fixed-power scopes as they might a television with no channel selector. But while variables give you flexibility (useful for people with only one rifle, but who want to hunt varmints and big game), they cost and weigh more and give you less latitude in ring spacing. You might find, as I did, that you settle on one power setting and rarely turn the dial.

Some hunters buy variables so they can crank them up to high power to glass a shaded draw or evaluate

## RETICLES

*Size, weight, brightness, magnification and size of objective lens are commonly discussed options in choosing a rifle scope. It is strange that the real business part of the scope, the reticle or crosshair that indicates the aiming point, gets less attention. Nine out of ten hunting scopes sold today have the plex reticle — crosshairs with thick sections leading to thinner lines near the intersection. Fine wires help precision shots at long range; the thicker sections can help find the crosshairs quickly in low light conditions or when the target is moving. Width of the thicker part of the plex reticle may vary by manufacturer.*

and require high rings. You just about need a sledge and a jack to get them into and out of scabbards. And the big glass helps you only at magnifications of 8X or higher in bad light.

An extralarge exit pupil can make shooting easier in bright light because it allows you to see a full field if your eye is a bit high, low or off to the side. That's why front bells make sense on 4X scopes. A straight tube with 22mm objective yields an exit pupil of 5.5 – adequate, if not ideal. A 32mm lens is much more forgiving when you must shoot quickly and your eye isn't centered.

Other scope terms include "relative brightness" (the exit pupil measurement squared) and "twilight factor" (the square root of the product of objective lens diameter and magnification). But exit pupil is all you really need to know when comparing similar scopes.

A 4X scope (or standard 6X, or a 2-7X or 2.5-8X variable) is light and trim enough to mount low. It shouldn't affect a rifle's balance. Popular 3-9X and 3.5-10X variables can make lightweight guns top-heavy. Straight-tube variables and fixed-power scopes, and the new compact models, are most appropriate for short, wispy guns. Last season I met a hunter carrying a six-pound rifle mated to a high-power variable scope. It fit like a cowbell on a cat.

On the other extreme, riflemen looking for top performance at any cost are buying European scopes with 30mm tubes. They're heavy and expensive: A 2.5-10X Zeiss weighs 24 ounces and lists for over $1400! In contrast, Bausch & Lomb's 2.5-10X scales 16 ounces and costs $653. It has an adjustable objective to correct for parallax (reticle displacement caused by off-center eye position).

Optical brilliance conceded, a big scope can be a poor choice, even when properly matched to a rifle. Not long ago a hunter came to elk camp lugging a rifle with a barrel the diameter of a truck axle, matched by a 12X scope. He expected to kill an elk far away. By hunt's end, he was wishing that gun had wheels. Puffing up a mountain, he muffed a

shot at a handsome bull at 250 yards – easy range for a practiced hunter with a hardware-store 30-06 and 4X scope.

## Customize Your Scope:

For years hunters have been told that long shots require huge scopes and rocketlike cartridges, that short shooting means iron sights and fat bullets. Sounds sensible. It isn't. Your hunting style, not hunting conditions, should guide your choice of gear.

One morning last fall I tiptoed into a whitetail covert and about an hour later shot a buck with my 30-06 Improved. It wore a 6X Leupold scope that helped me pick a path through the branches. I'm a deliberate shooter and would be ill-served by guns built for bounce-and-bang shots. That hefty Springfield and its open-country scope fit me. For the same reason I took an elk rifle to Zimbabwe and found it ideal. With that Model 70 and 4X scope I shot a big eland in dense bush at 20 yards and killed a galloping sable at 200.

How you use a scope is more important than its specifications. Proper mounting is the first step: the lower the better for quick aim and good gun balance. Many hunters mount their scopes too far back, pulling the tube to within three inches of their eye while standing as if at attention. In the woods, you may have to shoot quickly, thrusting your eye at the scope as you jam the rifle into your shoulder. A scope mounted well forward will bring the full field smoothly into view; one that protrudes too far to the rear will cost you time as you jockey your eye back and forth. If, like me, you crawl your stock, or if you must shoot prone or uphill, a protruding ocular housing will bang your brow on recoil. I position my hunting scopes with the ocular lens roughly 1/4 inch forward of the tang end of a Winchester Model 70, about even with the tail of the Remington 700's shorter tang. Your scope rifle and physique may indicate different placement.

Make sure the reticle is properly centered. After you've snugged one ring to hold the scope where you want it, put the rifle in sandbags and loosen

## ROUGH RANGEFINDER

*You can use the plex opening to roughly estimate range. Measure by sighting at a yardstick or check the manufacturer's literature to determine the opening measurement at 100 yards at a given power setting. If, for example, the opening covers 8 inches at 100 yards, a deer's top of back to bottom of chest (approx. 16 inches) that fits in the opening is standing at about 200 yards. If the deer fills half of the opening, he is nearly 400 yards away, an iffy shot for most hunters.*

the ring so you can rotate the scope and true up the reticle. Bring your head back behind the gun. You'll lose most of the field but see enough reticle to plumb the vertical wire with the buttplate. Throwing the rifle to your shoulder for a peek can give you a false sense of vertical.

Next, adjust the ocular lens so your reticle looks sharp. Do this by loosening the lock ring in front of the ocular housing and spinning it forward. Now thread the housing rearward. Pointing your rifle at the northern sky, look through the scope. The reticle should be fuzzy. Next, screw the ocular housing in one turn at a time until you see a sharp reticle. Don't stare! Your eye will automatically try to focus the reticle. When you get a sharp image instantly, tighten the lock ring.

"Sighting in" or zeroing is adjusting the scope so your line of sight coincides with the bullet's course at a given range. These paths cross twice; the second crossing is your zero range. I zero my big-game rifles at 200 yards regardless of cartridge or intended use. That way my bullets strike two to three inches high at 100 and drop six to 10 inches at 300, depending on the load. Holding spine-level on the shoulder of a buck last fall, I shot it through the lungs at 260 yards. A pronghorn two years ago fell to a lung shot at 380, my crosswire a hand-width above its withers.

Some hunters zero at 300 yards. They must then hold low between 150 and 200, where lots of game is shot. I prefer to hold over at long range, where I take fewer shots and usually have more time to figure out where to aim.

Rangefinding and lighted reticles and trajectory-compensation devices have never warmed my heart. To me, simple sight pictures and optical mechanisms are better than complicated ones.

Among reticles, my favorite is the plex. Its fine crosswire in the middle affords precise aim, while thick posts to the outside help in poor light and dense brush. I use the thin vertical wire below the intersection as a rangefinder by measuring its subtention at 100 yards.

I can then compare it to the body of an animal I'm aiming at and do some elementary math. If an 8-minute wire spans the depth of a buck's 20-inch chest, the range is about 250 yards.

This reticle can also serve as a trajectory compensator if its thin bottom-wire spans 6 to 8 minutes of angle. Say yours subtends seven inches. Instead of aiming with the intersection, you place the point of the lower post on the animal's brisket. That means at 100 yards you hit nine inches above it — a lung shot on deer or elk. At 200 yards the wire looks 14 inches long and your bullet hits at its top (the intersection), still inside the kill zone. At 300 yards the wire appears to span 21 inches, but your bullet has dropped eight, so you hit only 13 inches above the post. At 400, with a 28-inch subtention and 22-inch bullet drop, you drill the lungs yet again.

Finding a well-built scope is easy. Matching it to your rifle and hunting style, then mounting and adjusting it so it brings your line of sight and bullet together at the target, is time well spent. Practicing so you can use it effectively is downright essential.

## THE EYES HAVE IT

*Optimal eye relief – the distance between the shooter's eye and the ocular lens that provides a full sight picture – varies in both distance and latitude among scopes.*
*Critical eye relief means there's little margin for forward-and-back eye movement without shrinking the image boundary.*
*Parallax is apparent image displacement caused by the shooter's eye straying from the scope's axis.*
*Field of view is determined by both the size of the ocular lens and the magnification power of the scope.*

*Eye Relief*

P*roper scope mounting is critical. Set up for at least 3 inches of eye relief. Biscuit cuts on the eyebrow are bloody and painful.*

# Slug-Gunning for Deer

By Philip Bourjaily & Mike Bleech

*The new generation of dedicated guns and fine-tuned ammunition deliver accuracy and effectiveness unthinkable just five years ago.*

**S**erious riflemen, at least the ones I know, view slug guns with either polite disinterest or complete disdain. Yet as human populations grow and open spaces shrink, many of these same shooters will have to switch to shotguns someday or quit hunting deer.

That is not necessarily bad news. Manufacturers are turning out slug guns that look and shoot more like rifles than ever before. I myself, deservedly not a household name among bench shooters, recently put five slugs into 1⅞ inches at 100 yards with a BPS Game Gun. That's phenomenal accuracy when you consider the state of slug shooting just a few years ago.

### Slug-Gun Evolution:

Ithaca introduced the first dedicated slug gun in 1959, the Deerslayer version of its Model 37 pump. Its unrifled barrel was bored under-sized

to provide better accuracy with the smaller-diameter slugs of the time, and the rear sight ramp doubled as a scope base. Other manufacturers followed, turning out "buck specials" – standard bird guns with iron-sighted barrels.

During this era, whitetails were so scarce in much of slug-only country that few hunters pursued deer seriously enough to create a demand for better guns. Even just 10 years ago, minute-of-angle groups with slugs were unheard of; hunters boasted of guns that would put all their shots into a five-gallon milk can at 100 paces. Scopes had to be jerry-rigged onto most shotguns and rifled barrels were a curiosity. Most hunters simply squinted down the rib of a duck gun at their annual deer.

During the 1960s and '70s, however, whitetail populations exploded and deer hunter numbers rose. As more areas were legislated off-limits to rifles, the market for improved slug guns grew. In the early 1980s, slug guns garnered the attention of gunsmiths, foremost among them Ole Oleson at E.R. Shaw, a California shop specializing in Mauser conversions. Shaw rifled barrels soon became (and still are) available as custom jobs on solid-frame shotguns. Shortly thereafter, Bob Rott and Phil Frigon of Kansas jumped into the rifled-bore business with their Hastings "Paradox" interchangeable barrels. All of a sudden, hunters could buy a rifled Hastings barrel for their bird gun and simply swap barrels when deer season rolled around.

## The New Era:

The Mossberg Trophy Slugster, introduced in 1987, was the first production rifled-barrel slug gun. Fitted with an extended scope mount on the rifled barrel and a high-comb stock designed especially for use with telescopic sights, the Mossberg set the pattern for a new generation of slug guns. Remington followed with its cantilever mount 11-87s and 870s, as did Ithaca with the solid-frame Deerslayer II, Browning with its BPS Game Gun and Winchester with the 1300. All are shooters capable of two- to five-inch groups at 100 yards with sabot ammunition; both the Browning and Winchester successfully flout the long-standing rule that a gun with a removable barrel must have a mount on the barrel to shoot well.

Today numerous manufacturers make dedicated 12-gauge pump and autoloading slug guns, and they're beginning to dabble in 20-gauge models. Almost all the new guns feature sling swivels and stock dimensions suitable for scopes and iron sights. Unfortunately, most leave the factory with the same (read: heavy, creepy, bad) trigger that goes on bird guns. Manufacturers will likely address this problem in time. Meanwhile, Hastings has introduced adjustable rifle-type triggers for Remington 12 gauges, with other models to follow. In addition, Hastings offers an ever-increasing line of rifled barrels with scope mounts or iron sights.

Several manufacturers offer models with rifled screw-in tubes for hunters who'd like one gun to shoot both slugs and standard shotshells. The jury remains out on most rifled tubes; in theory, they shouldn't work, since the slug is already traveling at top speed when it meets the grooves. But everyone, myself included, who's tested Browning's extra-long (five-inch) rifled choke tube has been amazed to find it shoots as well as many fully rifled barrels.

The latest logical development of the slug-shooting shotgun occurred to Pennsylvanian Randy Fritz, who reasoned: If a shotgun is going to be used as a rifle, why shouldn't it *be* a rifle? Legally and semantically, Fritz's Tar-Hunt is a shotgun, since it is chambered for shotshells, but it yields riflelike performance thanks to a free-floated Shaw barrel,

a solid bolt-action lockup, a rifle-type stock and a fine trigger. Fritz, a competitive bench shooter, has recorded minute-of-angle groups with the Tar-Hunt. Last year Marlin introduced its own bolt-action slug gun and Browning announced the A-Bolt Shotgun, which reached dealers' shelves this year. Another new gun with intriguing accuracy potential is the H&R 980, a single-shot, break-open gun fitted with what is essentially a varmint barrel in 12 gauge.

In 10 years, shotguns have evolved from milk-can-at-40-paces accuracy to the point where a modern rifled slug gun with sabot ammunition will allow a skilled shooter to take deer to 125 yards. That's hardly a new concept for deer rifles, but for slug guns, it's a revolutionary idea indeed.

## Slug Types:

Shotgun slugs that are currently available can be grouped into three categories: sabot, trailing wad and full-bore. All three are capable of 125-yard accuracy when matched with the proper slug gun.

Sabot slugs revolutionized slug shooting during the 1980s. The slugs themselves are smaller than the bore diameter, which allows for a more ballistically efficient shape. The two-piece sabot encasing the slug is large enough to engage the rifling of a modern slug barrel, thus imparting a stabilizing spin to the slug. After the slug leaves the barrel the sabot separates and drops away. Sabot slugs are generally best suited to rifled barrels — especially those with a relatively fast twist rate of 1 in 27 to 34 inches — yet shoot accurately through some smoothbore barrels. Rifled choke tubes produce surprisingly good accuracy.

A full-bore slug has a concave base, which expands when fired so it will fit the bore diameter of the barrel through which it is traveling. Since shotgun barrels vary considerably in diameter, no specific slug diameter would fit all barrels tightly. Full-bore slugs are comparatively wide and short, and are more accurate in rifled barrels with slow twist rates of 1 in 34 to 36 inches.

Most full-bore slugs are termed "rifled" slugs because the slugs themselves have lands and grooves on their outer surfaces. This rifled appearance lends the assumption that the slug spins when fired through a smoothbore barrel, but such is not the case. Yet this "rifling" does promote the slug's expansion to bore size in both rifled and smoothbore barrels.

The traditional American full-bore slug, the Foster style, was designed long ago for use in smoothbore barrels. Although their style has not changed much, they still perform surprisingly well in modern slug barrels. I have gotten acceptable accuracy — three shots inside six inches at 125 yards — with all major brands.

On a trailing wad slug, the wad is attached to the slug itself to improve stabilization in flight. Trailing wad slugs can also be of the sabot and full-bore categories and are suitable for rifled barrels, smoothbores or rifled choke tubes. Most of these slugs perform better in barrels with a slower rifling twist.

## By Hand:

Until recently, handloading slugs was a rather complicated process. Finding tools and components was difficult. Now a series of Buckbuster Shotgun Bullets from S.G.B. Manufacturing has made it relatively easy. Currently available only in 12 gauge, these slugs use standard shot cups as sabots. Combining the best of sabot and full-bore slugs' best features, they can be loaded in most shotshell presses without modification. My tests have shown superb accuracy: three-shot, four-inch groups at 150 yards.

## Results from the Range:

Shotgun slugs have a short range and a low likelihood of ricochet. These two unchanging ballistic factors are precisely why more and more areas of high human population density are coming under "slug only" big-game hunting regulations.

What has changed significantly about slugs is their maximum *effective* range. A slug is still ballistically inferior to a rifle bullet, however, and two critical factors — trajectory and the effect of wind — rule out most slug-shooting at game beyond 125 yards.

A typical slug, fired from a gun parallel to the ground at shoulder height, will travel only about 240 yards. Tests of a variety of 12-gauge sabot slugs show an average drop of six inches between 125 and 150 yards (with sights zeroed at 100 yards). So a shooter's estimation of the distance to a faraway target must be close to exact. Misjudging the range by as few as 15 yards could lead to a miss or, worse, a wounded animal.

Many slug hunters mistakenly assume that wind does not have a large effect on slug accuracy. However, a mild breeze destroys accuracy beyond 125 yards; a stiff wind makes shooting beyond 75 yards difficult. Shooting straight into the wind is just as unpredictable.

When testing the maximum effective range of modern slugs, I fired several loads through two guns: a Tar-Hunt RSG-12 and a Browning BPS fitted with a Hastings rifled barrel. When there was absolutely no wind, two factory loads (Lightfield 1¼-ounce sabot slugs and Remington 12-gauge Copper Solid sabot slugs) consistently produced three-shot groups smaller than six inches at 200 yards in both slug guns. The following day, in gusty wind, I could not even keep the slugs on my 30x48-inch target frames.

## SELECTED FACTORY SLUG LOADS

### Sabot

- Federal Premium Sabot Slugs: 12 gauge 1 ounce; 20 gauge ⅝ ounce.
- Remington Copper Solid Sabot Slugs: 12 gauge 1 ounce, 1³⁄₁₆ ounce; 20 gauge ¾ ounce.
- Winchester Super-X BRI Hollow Point Sabot Slugs: 12 gauge 1 ounce; 20 gauge ⅝ ounce.

### Full-Bore

- Federal Classic Rifled Slugs: 10 gauge 1¾ ounces; 12 gauge 1¼ ounces, 1 ounce; 16 gauge ⅘ ounce; 20 gauge ¾ ounce; 410 bore ⅕ ounce.
- Remington Slugger Rifled Slugs: 12 gauge 1 ounce; 16 gauge ⅘ ounce; 20 gauge ⅝ ounce; 410 bore ⅕ ounce.
- Winchester Super-X Hollow Point Rifled Slugs: 12 gauge 1 ounce; 16 gauge ⅘ ounce; 20 gauge ¾ ounce; 410 bore ⅕ ounce.

### Trailing Wad

- ACTIV Premium Slugs: 12 gauge 1 ounce, 1¼ ounces; 20 gauge ⅞ ounce.
- Fiocchi Hollow Point Rifled Slugs: 12 gauge 1 ounce; 1¼ ounces.
- Rottweil Brenneke 3-inch magnum: 12 gauge 1⅜ ounces; 20 gauge 1 ounce; 410 bore ¼ ounce.

### Trailing Wad/Sabot

- Lightfield Hybred EXP-Sabot Slugs: 12 gauge 1¼ ounces.

### Trailing Wad/Full-Bore

- Rottweil Brenneke Golden Slugs: 12 gauge 490 grains; 16 gauge 415 grains; 20 gauge 370 grains.

# The *Troubled Shooter*

*By Aaron Fraser Pass*

*How to determine the problems — and fix them —
when your sighting-in session goes sour.*

A scoped big-game rifle is an integrated system of many different parts and materials. All of them must work together for successful sighting-in and reliable accuracy. But even if your deer rifle hasn't shifted its zero since the Nixon administration, things happen to change that: Scopes get bumped; screws work loose; wood stocks swell and warp; the cartridge box with the 1776-1976 Bicentennial logo is empty and you buy new ammo. All can change your point of impact radically.

To solve an accuracy problem, you first must make sure your sighting-in procedure itself isn't causing it.

## Sight-In Prerequisites:

**1** - Always shoot from a stable platform. A solid benchrest, with sandbags or a shooting cradle, is best. Shooting over rolled-up sleeping bags or car hoods is barely better than no rest at all.

**2** - Start with an adequate supply of the same ammunition brand and bullet weight. Most rifles shoot different loads and bullets to different places.

**3** - Tighten up scope-mounting and stock-bedding screws before you shoot. Loose screws cause bad groups or no group at all. Changing screw tension, particularly the bedding screws, also changes the point of impact.

**4** - Wear eye and ear protection (required on most rifle ranges). All deer-class firearms report in the ear-damaging decibel level. Such protection also reduces the possibility of flinching.

**5** - Clean the bore, then shoot a couple of rounds through it before settling down to sight-in. Most rifles shoot a "flyer" or two from a freshly cleaned barrel. Sometimes they're off only a little bit...but sometimes they're off a lot.

**6** - There comes a point of diminishing returns during every sighting-in session. When fatigue and/or frustration take over, you are wasting ammunition and probably developing a flinch. Stop shooting and come back another day for a fresh start, with fresh thinking.

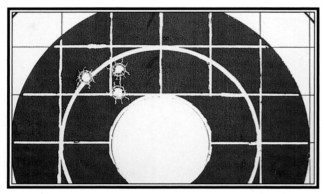
*Good group*

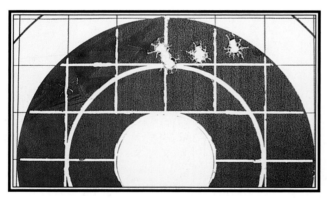
*Shot stringing*

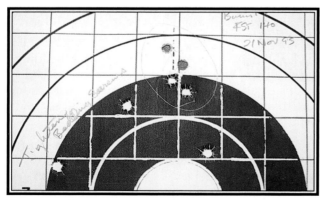
*Loose grouping*

## The Procedure:

Shoot three or more shots at the target from a steady rest. Many hunting rifles have rather thin barrels to reduce weight, but they heat up quickly. Let the barrel cool for a few minutes between shots to get a true picture of first-shot performance.

The bullets should land in an even cluster, or a group. Do not adjust sights on the basis of a single shot, which is not a proper indication of where the rifle is actually shooting. Many perfectly sighted-in rifles have been literally screwed out of zero when one wild shot caused the shooter to adjust prematurely.

Measure the vertical and horizontal distance from the group to your desired point of impact. Turn the scope adjustments the correct number of clicks (read the scope instructions) in the correct direction (read the arrows). In a perfect world, you should now be sighted in. Unfortunately, the world is frequently imperfect.

## The Good Gun Gone Bad:

A formerly accurate rifle that suddenly shoots poorly is perplexing. "Suddenly" is the key word. Don't automatically assume that the barrel is excessively worn or "shot-out" if group size abruptly enlarges. A worn barrel loses accuracy gradually.

First, check for damage to the rifling at the muzzle crown. A simple recrowning job by a gunsmith will fix that.

Next, look for loose scope-mount or bedding screws. Use special gunsmithing screwdrivers ground to fit the unique taper of gun-screw slots. Standard household screwdrivers will ruin gun-screw heads.

Also clean the bore with a specialized copper-removing agent. These chemical solutions are much stronger than standard gun-cleaning solvents. Read and follow the directions to prevent damage to your rifle or to yourself. After a severe cleaning, the bore must recondition itself, so don't panic if the first shots after cleaning show little improvement.

If there is still no change, the next logical suspicion is wood-stock warpage or a change in the bedding. Read the groups to figure it out.

## Reading the Group:

A rifle is like a tuning fork. The whole rig, and especially the barrel, begins to vibrate as soon as the sear slips. This vibration intensifies as the firing pin falls, the primer pops, the powder burns and the bullet spins out of the barrel. A rifle that resonates uniformly with each shot produces small, even groups. Three-shot groups should print a relatively even triangle (*see top photo at left*); five or more shots should be evenly spaced and round. Anything interfering with this harmonic vibration enlarges or distorts the group.

Vertical or horizontal lines of bullet holes — "shot stringing" — usually indicate a warped stock putting uneven pressure on the barrel. If the first two or three shots group well and subsequent shots "walk" out of group as the barrel heats up (*middle photo*), barrel-channel bedding is the probable culprit. (Knowing the sequence of shot placement is important. A spotting scope can save many trips to the target frame.)

Loose or irregular grouping is often the product of bad action bedding or an out-of-line barreled action. "Two-grouping" (the rifle shoots two distinct groups with the same sight setting) is usually an action-bedding problem. This may be cured (*bottom photo*) by tightening action screws — or it may require an expert bedding job or a "truing" of the barreled action.

## The Adjustment Period:

Modern telescopic sights are noteworthy for their ruggedness and reliability. However, older scopes (like older people) may get set in their ways. The reticle may stick and not move when the adjustment dial is turned. Lightly tapping the adjustment dial may help. Usually the recoil from the first shot shakes the reticle loose and into its new position. Don't be too quick to adjust if the first shot from a new sight setting goes into the original group.

Adjustment consistency is important. Many good scopes may not move the group the exact distance indicated in the instructions. That's no big deal if all the graduations adjust the same amount. If one click means so much and the next click means something different, however, that's a problem. A scope with uneven, unreliable adjustments is difficult to impossible to zero. Return that scope to the manufacturer for correction.

A scope's reticle can be adjusted only so far. Read the instructions to determine the total vertical and horizontal adjustment range of a new scope. If you must make excessive adjustment (more than two-thirds of half the total adjustment range) or completely run out of adjustment while trying to bore-sight or sight-in, suspect incompatible scope mounts and bases, incorrect scope mounting or even out-of-line mounting holes drilled into the rifle's receiver.

## Prep for New Rifles:

Before shooting a new rifle (or an older rifle with a new scope), bore-sight it and start off at short range to "get on paper." To bore-sight a bolt-action, remove the bolt, rest the rifle firmly, and visually center the bore on a distant object. Next, adjust the crosshairs onto that object. An optical device called a collimator bore-sights all action types by aligning the bore with a screen for crosshair adjustment.

At the range, set your first target at 25 or 50 yards. Remember: The scope's adjustments are proportionately fractionalized at these distances. A scope "click" that equates to $1/2$ inch at 100 yards equals $1/4$ inch at 50 yards and only $1/8$ inch at 25.

Once the rifle is shooting where you want it at short range, set a target out at 100 yards and shoot. In theory, short-range sighting-in is possible because the bullet's trajectory is known and predictable. In practice, though, human error factors in. Just as scope adjustments are fractionalized by short range, bullet dispersion is magnified by long range. Group size (and error) doubles as range doubles. If the exact center of a bullet hole is $1/2$ inch off at 25 yards, that bullet will be 1 inch off at 50, 2 inches off at 100 and 4 inches off at 200 yards. Short-range sighting-in requires very precise measurement and careful calculation.

Owners of brand-new rifles often are initially disappointed by mediocre accuracy. New rifles, like new cars, require a "break-in" for optimum performance. The barreled action must settle into its bedding. Also, the first bullets sent down a brand-new bore actually lap (polish) it, resulting in a different point of impact. Kenny Jarrett, custom maker of the ultra-accurate Beanfield rifles in Jackson, South Carolina, recommends cleaning the bore after each of the first 20 shots for optimal accuracy.

# The Muzzleloading Revolution

*By Gerald Almy*

A *flintlock, the traditional blackpowder rifle.*

*Primitive and modern blackpowder disciplines are sweeping the country — and adding a whole new element to the chase.*

**O**n Mt. Taylor in central New Mexico, Jim Kohl races through a field of tall brown grass, cutting the distance to the elk bugling in the ponderosa pines. Catching his breath, he kneels, picks a spot on the bull 100 yards away and touches the trigger. A plume of blue smoke belches into the thin mountain air. The conical lead bullet drops the 6x6, which will later score 322 Boone and Crockett points.

In the Blue Ridge Mountains of Virginia, Jim Smith watches a doe slip down the trail toward him. The sight buoys his spirits after a long, quiet day in the woods — he knows the rut is in and feels certain a buck will follow the doe. And he's right. Smith's muzzleloader roars and the largest nontypical whitetail ever taken with a blackpowder rifle is down — a 35-pointer that scores 259⅞.

In a northern Manitoba thicket, Ed Brummel waits on a tree stand with his 50-caliber muzzleloader in his hands. Three hours into the afternoon hunt, he hears a "whoof" 15 yards away. A bear is staring at him. In seconds, the bruin approaches the stand, rises on its hind legs and reaches toward him. The bear's paws come to the fifth rung of the seven-rung ladder. Eventually the bruin drops down and starts to move away. Brummel regains his composure quickly, takes aim and shoots. The 300-pound bear runs 25 yards and lies still.

The reasons these hunters chose blackpowder firearms for their hunts are as varied as the reasons for hunting itself. The sheer adrenaline rush of pursuing big game with a primitive, one-shot gun is certainly a motivation, but there are also many practical purposes for taking up muzzleloading:

Special Hunting Areas: Kohl hunted one of several huge hunting areas in New Mexico reserved exclusively for muzzleloader elk hunters. Hundreds of other areas in the West are off-limits to modern-rifle hunters, but open to those carrying muzzleloaders. Many contain particularly high populations of trophy elk and deer.

Prime Hunting Periods: Smith took his huge whitetail by watching a doe's trail for a rutting buck, a time-proven method. Bow season opens before the rut in many areas, and rifle season often comes after its peak. But in Smith's hunting area, and in many others across the country, early muzzleloader hunts coincide exactly with the height of rutting activity for deer, elk and antelope.

Extra Challenge: This is what drove

Brummel to carry a single-shot, close-range blackpowder gun instead of a scoped modern rifle to the woods of Manitoba, and it's what encourages many blackpowder hunters to take up the sport. Squeezing off on a deer, bear or elk with a multi-shot rifle from 200 yards with a high-powered scope has lost luster for some hunters; going afield with a primitive firearm adds fresh challenge. You have to hunt harder, smarter and more patiently, developing greater woods skills and learning more about the quarry, to deliver one close, accurate shot.

Longer Seasons: Extra muzzleloader seasons mean more hunting time. Many states schedule blackpowder seasons before modern-firearms hunts; some have them after; other have them both before and after. Where I live in Virginia, I can hunt deer 12 days with

## PRIMERS

*Some in-line muzzleloaders now are manufactured, or can be retrofitted with a conversion kit, to use shotgun or centerfire rifle primers providing hotter ignition than percussion caps.*

*M*odern in-line muzzleloaders are popular with the majority of today's blackpowder hunters.

## SWAB IT OUT

*Following each shot on the range, run a clean moist patch down the barrel with your cleaning jag to remove the powder residue. Fouling buildup in the barrel adversely affects accuracy and makes subsequent projectiles increasingly harder to load.*

a modern firearm and 30 other days with a blackpowder rifle.

Less-Skittish Game: Since there are fewer blackpowder hunters than modern-firearm hunters, there's less pressure on the animals during muzzleloader seasons. You'll see more animals moving in a natural manner, allowing you to pattern their feeding and bedding habits with less chance of other hunters interfering with your strategy or spoiling your solitude.

Increased Bag: Many states offer tags to take additional deer if you buy a muzzleloader license.

Rekindled Roots: Blackpowder hunting provides a sense of connection with our forefathers and the challenges that early frontiersmen faced.

Intensified Drama: Muzzleloaders enhance the excitement of the hunt because of the close range involved. There's no question that an encounter with a buck, bear or bull elk at 50 yards is more exciting than aiming at the same animal through a cranked-up scope at 250 yards. My closest blackpowder kill was a 300-pound wild bear taken at four yards. That was exciting.

These are also some of the reasons muzzleloading is the fastest-growing hunting sport in America today. According to estimates by the National Muzzleloading Rifle Association, 1 million people shot black powder a decade ago; today, 3 million do. The types of muzzleloaders and the gear for them have increased – and, in some cases, changed – as well. If you're interested in pursuing the sport, here are the basics:

### The Rifles:

Most blackpowder rifles shoot farther than many hunters can accurately aim them. Shot groups of one to two inches at 50 yards and two to four inches at 100 yards are common. For the majority of hunters using iron sights, 60 to 75 yards is a good practical maximum range in the field. If your state allows scopes on muzzleloaders and you are an excellent shot, you can take game out to 125 yards.

A 54-caliber blackpowder rifle shooting a 425-grain conical bullet has about 1300 foot-pounds of energy at 100 yards – almost as much energy as a 170-grain bullet fired from a 30-30 at

that range. Blackpowder firearms can drop game quickly and humanely; the farthest I ever tracked an animal I shot with a blackpowder rifle was 50 yards. Many fell on the spot.

Flintlock rifles, which were invented in 1615, use two different sizes of black powder. A coarse-grained powder (size FFg) is poured down the barrel; a finer powder (FFFFg) is put in the pan. When you pull the trigger, an exposed flint strikes a steel frizzen, producing a shower of sparks that ignite the powder in the pan. This throws a flame through the flash hole and into the breech, igniting the barrel powder and sending the bullet toward its target.

In 1807 the percussion rifle was developed. It employs a small cap that fits onto a nipple outside the breech. A hammer strikes the cap when you pull the trigger, which sends a flame through the flash hole and into the barrel, igniting the coarse barrel powder.

The majority of blackpowder hunters choose percussion rifles, as flintlocks are more tedious to use and more prone to misfire. (Pennsylvania is the only state that mandates the use of flintlocks during its special blackpowder season.) A few hunters use long-barreled rifles that are historical replicas of Kentucky-style guns, but far more choose short-barreled firearms that are lighter to carry, easier to maneuver in brush and just as accurate. Barrel lengths of 21 to 28 inches are typical.

Replica flintlock and percussion guns are sidelocks, meaning the hammer is mounted on the side of the gun. In-line ignition rifles – first popularized by the Modern Muzzleloading's Knight MK-85 but now available from other manufacturers such as CVA, Navy Arms, Remington, Thompson/Center, Traditions and White – are similar to modern bolt-action rifles in feel and appearance. They feature a spring-powered striker that drives forward directly in line with the bore, speeding ignition.

The 45 caliber was once considered the standard muzzleloader size for deer. It will still perform adequately, but most hunters prefer the 50 or 54 caliber, either of which is powerful enough for bear, elk, moose, wild boar and antelope as well.

Many states still require the use of

## DRY FIRING PRIMERS

*Push a clean patch on a cleaning jag completely down the barrel before dry firing caps to clear out the nipple and breech plug. Some percussion caps sound like a good fire, but they can leave a residue that plugs the nipple. The small back-blast from the percussion charge hitting the jag should clean out any residue. A burn mark on the clean patch absolutely verifies that ignition made it through the nipple and breech plug.*

*Hunter firing a flintlock muzzleloader*

iron sights on blackpowder rifles during muzzleloading seasons, but some now allow scopes. Greater accuracy in aiming and increased light-gathering ability makes scopes a good investment where legal. Choose a variable – 1.5-6X, 2-7X or 3-9X.

### The Ammunition:

Round balls are the least powerful blackpowder projectiles you can use. They require patching and lubrication and are becoming less popular with hunters every year. A round ball shot from a 50-caliber blackpowder rifle carries only about 400 foot-pounds of energy at 100 yards.

Conical bullets weigh about twice as much as a round ball of the same caliber and deliver nearly double the energy down range. Examples include the CVA Deerslayer, Thompson/Center Maxi-Hunter, Buffalo Bullet and Hornady Great Plains. They require lubrication.

The third type of projectile is a saboted bullet such as those made by Barnes, Muzzleload Magnum, Buffalo, Hornady, Thompson/Center, CVA, Nosler and others. These allow the use of a variety of projectiles, including modern jacketed pistol bullets and others made exclusively for muzzleloaders. A plastic sleeve, which holds the bullet and seals the bore, falls away after the projectile leaves the barrel. Sabots are

the most accurate of all in some guns, but lack the heavier weight of pure lead bullets. Not allowed in blackpowder seasons of some states, saboted bullets do not require lubricants.

The best degree of rifling, or rate of twist, differs for each projectile. Round balls require a slow rate of twist, around 1:66 (one turn in 66 inches). Conical bullets and those in sabots perform better with a fast twist, something in the 1:20 or 1:32 range. If you shoot both bullets and balls, choose a compromise twist such as 1:48.

Most muzzleloading rifles shoot best with FFg blackpowder (the fewer the Fs, the coarser the powder). Substitute powders such as Pyrodex® and the new Black Canyon are popular because they require less cleanup. (Note: Never use modern smokeless powder in muzzleloaders. The guns are not designed to withstand the pressures generated by smokeless powder.)

### Necessary Gear:

A short starter is used to push the bullet into the muzzle, where it is first engraved by the lands. A ramrod is then used to drive the bullet down and seat it firmly against the powder charge. It's a good idea to notch your ramrod after ensuring that the ball is seated against the powder, so you will know how far to push the ball when loading in the future.

A graduated cylinder measure is useful for premeasuring charges of black powder. You can load powder directly into the gun with one, or put each measured load in a quick loader for fast access in the field. Most quick-loading devices, such as those by Butler Creek, hold a bullet and two percussion caps as well as the powder charge, for fast reloading after the initial shot. Carry three or four such quick loaders in your pocket when hunting.

Percussion caps vary in size. Most muzzleloaders take a Size 11 cap, but some brands fit certain guns better than others. Experiment to see which works best with your rifle. When hunting, it's wise to carry a spare nipple, a nipple wrench, and a pick to clean the opening.

Likewise, flints vary in size and quality. Flintlock hunters should carry spare flints and a pick to clean the flash hole. Some muzzleloader hunters use a possibles bag to carry their gear. I find it much more efficient to keep specific items in certain pockets so I can get to them quickly and easily.

### Finding the Perfect Load:

Before loading powder, fire two percussion caps without a load to clear the barrel of oil residue. Flintlock hunters should dry fire to check for proper spark.

Start with a light load, slowly working up to increase power while maintaining accuracy. With a 50-caliber rifle, for example, start with 50 grains of FFg black powder, then increase to 60, 70, etc. Eventually you'll find the best amount of powder for your particular rifle. I shoot 54-caliber guns and find 100 to 110 grains optimal for lead conical bullets. For lighter sabot bullets, 85 to 90 grains is the maximum recommended charge. (Never exceed the manufacturer's recommendations for powder.)

Sight-in initially at 13 yards. This may sound close, but it will put a typical blackpowder rifle one to two inches high at 25 yards, two to three inches high at 50 yards, one to two inches high at 75 yards, dead on at 90 to 100 yards and three to five inches low at 125 yards. With this system you don't have to hold high or low at any target out to just over 100 yards. Beyond that, few of us should shoot at game with a muzzleloader.

Allow some time to familiarize yourself with all the loading and firing steps. Blackpowder guns have a slower lock time than do cartridge guns, and you'll need to practice shooting to become proficient.

Blackpowder rifles are magnets for rust, so you must clean the gun thoroughly after each use. Special solvents are available, or you can use soap and hot water until the barrel comes clean and exposed metal parts are free of fouling. Dry the gun and add a very light coat of oil or lubricant to all metal parts.

## SHOOTING

## POUR NO MORE

*Tired of messing with a powder measure and flask, pouring powder from a quickload on your boots instead of down the barrel? Hodgden Powder Co. has come up with an answer to the powder-spilling woes for shooters with in-line muzzleloaders. They've found a way to mold Pyrodex®, their synthetic black powder, into measured 50-grain pellets. For a 100-grain load, just drop two pills down the barrel, stuff in whatever projectile, cap it and it's ready to go.*

*Advantages of the Pyrodex® pellets (below) include convenience and consistency; they seem to burn cleaner than the other powders, leaving less residue in the barrel after each shot.*

## GOING TO EXTREMES

*When blackpowder guns were first reintroduced to the hunting world in the late 1960s, they were strict re-creations of guns used 100 to 200 years ago. Authenticity and immersing oneself in the past were the goals. This buck-skinner approach is still popular with a small segment of blackpowder shooters, but most hunters today are more pragmatic. They have entered the sport because of the increased opportunity to pursue game. These hunters see muzzleloading as an extension of their regular hunting and have demanded more modernized versions of guns, optics and bullets. The result has been a dramatic restructuring of blackpowder hunting equipment. Scopes, in-line ignitions, plastic-saboted bullets, short barrels, faster twist rates and synthetic stocks are some of the utilitarian changes hunters have embraced. Neither extreme is superior, however, and many hunters – by choice or by law – choose positions in the middle of this spectrum.*

# Handgunning for Deer

*By Tom Gresham*

*F*ollowing an increase in pistol target shooting participation, the use of handguns for hunting deer has become a popular option for many hunters.

*The power and accuracy of these guns could surprise you.*

**C**ontrary to the common line parroted by much of the media, handguns are accurate, sporting and fun to shoot. Some of the handguns used by deer hunters are, in fact, capable of astounding accuracy at truly impressive ranges.

Hunters gravitate toward handguns for much the same reason they take up archery and muzzleloading — as a way to put an extra challenge into hunting and to have new equipment and skills to master.

As deer hunters started to take up handguns, some of them weren't satisfied with iron-sighted revolvers. They developed new guns and new cartridges, special sights and accessories that far surpass anything the old-time pistoleros ever dreamed of.

## Scope Your Handgun:

Handguns are not inherently inaccurate, but the short sight radius makes aiming with iron sights difficult. Scope sights eliminate that problem, giving the same benefits as they do on a rifle or shotgun — a single image plane and simplicity in aiming.

At first, handgun scopes were low-power models that suited short-range revolver cartridges. With the advent of long-range cartridges in handguns, hunters needed more magnification. Scope makers responded by bringing out long-eye-relief, variable-power scopes that top out at 7 or 8 power.

High-power scopes and long-range cartridges require a steady rest, and it's not unusual to see a handgun wearing a bipod. A handgun chambered for a cartridge such as the 7mm-08, with a good scope and a bipod, makes 250-yard shots at deer practical for a good shooter. To determine your maximum hunting range, shoot 10 shots at a round paper plate. The distance where you can consistently put nine out of 10 shots on the paper, from a hunting-style rest, is your maximum.

## The Versatile Contender:

One handgun, the single-shot, break-action Thompson/Center Contender, has brought thousands into the ranks of handgun hunters. By switching between the wide assortment of inter-changeable barrels, a hunter can shoot any number of pistol and rifle cartridges in a single Contender frame. The action is simple, strong and accurate, and it makes scope mounting easy. Barrels are available for cartridges from 22 rimfire to the 30-30 Winchester, 35 Remington, and 45-70.

When even the Contender isn't enough, take a look at SSK Industries, the "handcannon" firm created by noted handgun hunter J.D. Jones. SSK starts with a Contender frame, then mounts a custom barrel chambered for a powerful factory or wildcat cartridge capable of taking the largest game or shooting at distances of hundreds of yards.

The first popular bolt-action handgun was the exotic-looking Remington XP-100, which was initially chambered for the 221

Fireball. Now the XP comes in several flavors, in composite and wood stocks, in varmint calibers as well as big-game rounds like the 7mm-08 and even the 350 Remington Magnum, and in single-shot and repeater versions.

Other companies that make bolt-action or break-open handguns suitable for hunting include McMillan, Anschütz, Wichita Arms, Magnum Research, Ultra Light Arms and Pachmayr.

If you want magnum power in a modern revolver, consider the Freedom Arms 454 Casull. It's a big, stainless-steel, single-shot revolver chambered for the potent 454 Casull cartridge, which delivers more energy at 100 yards than the 44 magnum does at the muzzle.

What calibers are best for deer hunting? The 41 magnum and the venerable 44 magnum are good ones. In the long-range calibers, some of the better choices include the 7mm BR Rem, any of the JDJ wildcat cartridges, 7-30 Waters, 7mm-08 Rem, 30 Herrett, 30-30 Win, and anything bigger that you can shoot accurately.

## Hunting Tactics:

The strategy for hunting deer with a handgun is the same as with a rifle, shotgun or bow. Scout the area well and set up to give yourself the closest shot possible. Forget jump-shooting or any kind of deer drives that are likely to result in running shots. With a handgun, you want a stationary target, and you should use a rest for your gun whenever possible.

Before heading afield with your hand-gun, check the state and local laws, not just hunting regulations. You may be required to carry that gun locked in the trunk. Also, if you hunt with the gun in a holster, don't forget to take it off when you get back to your vehicle.

*Good cartridges for handguns used by deer hunters, from left: 35 Rem, 30-30 Win, 7mm-08 Rem, and 44 Rem Mag.*

## SHORT-BARRELED RIFLES?

*No, handguns! However, the Remington XP-100, introduced in 1963, started a modern revolution in the way of viewing handguns. Other manufacturers have developed their own models, providing a choice to long-range handgun fanciers. With a 10- to 16-inch barrel, bolt or break-down action, sporting a scope and chambered for large centerfire calibers, these modern handguns can shoot much less than one-inch groups at 100 yards. The effective hunting range of these weapons extends well beyond 100 yards. Ways have been found to improve both range and accuracy of these weapons, spurred partly by their use in competition.*

*Are long-range hand-guns new? Certainly not. The Colt "Buntline Special" revolver with an attachable shoulder stock, 16-inch barrel, firing what was probably a 44-40 caliber, dates back to the late 1800s.*

# Get That Bow Out of the Closet

*By Dwight Schuh*

*A bowhunter who takes his tackle out just before the season is making a big mistake.*

## ACCURACY

*Having accuracy problems? Perhaps using a release aid will help. Advantages of a release aid are: It grips the string at one point, insuring a smooth, crisp release every time. It's unaffected by cold, fatigue and other conditions. Finally, it can (and should) surprise you when it goes off, a key element in accuracy.*

Even as a bow sits in a closet, its synthetic cables and strings may stretch, especially in hot weather, and small amounts of stretch will alter the point of arrow impact. Thus, you cannot assume that a bow hitting dead on before storage will be hitting in the same place after storage. You must practice well ahead of the season to confirm or to readjust sight settings.

Additionally, with any extended layoff, you, the shooter, will get stale. I would compare shooting a bow with swinging a golf club, because performance depends largely on the human element. A golfer, for example, must continually work on conditioning, form, timing and rhythm to maintain his level of play. The same concept applies to archers. Experienced bowhunters should practice regularly for at least a month before the season; novices, two months or more.

If you alter tackle or form, devote even more time. Many years ago I changed my style slightly two weeks before the season, which seemed no problem since the new style came easily. When shooting at a deer, however, I unconsciously reverted to my old style – and blew the shot. I've seen other hunters make similar mistakes.

If you plan to change anything, do it well before hunting season.

## Shooting Well:

I recently visited Browning pro-staff shooter Randy Ulmer, a top 3-D archer and hunter. During some friendly competition, I said, "Don't you let me beat you just to make me feel good." He laughed. "Not a chance."

His competitive nature wouldn't allow that, but his response also suggested a practice ethic. "I always shoot to the best of my ability," Ulmer explained. "My strongest practice philosophy is that I never shoot an arrow without a purpose. With each shot I'm working on some aspect of my form – my bow hand, relaxation, aiming. I won't shoot an arrow just to shoot it.

"If you practice mediocre shots, you'll be a mediocre archer. You don't have to practice a lot to do real well. If you practice shooting every arrow right, you'll develop the good habits needed to shoot well under any conditions."

Dave Holt, archery instructor and technical editor for *Bowhunter* magazine, said, "Commonly, people who come to my school have to warm up first, and then they start shooting well. They

*B*efore the season opener you should practice shooting from a tree stand to familiarize yourself with arrow trajectory at different distances.

might say, 'What do you think of that?' I say, 'I'm not interested in your good arrows. I'm interested in your worst arrows.' A hunter may get only one shot — so that first shot must count."

### Dress Rehearsal:

Not long ago, another magazine ran a story in which the author had practiced with field points all summer and then screwed broadheads onto his arrows just before the season. He'd never shot the broadheads, and then, to his surprise, his first shot at a deer careened off target. You can't assume broadheads will fly like field points Most won't. Practice with them.

Shoot in your hunting clothes, too. Practicing in a bulky coat, facemask and heavy gloves is nothing like doing it in shorts and a tank top. Don't wait until a buck is 20 yards from your tree stand to discover the difference.

Dress rehearsals should also include such variables as wind, fatigue, varied

angles and awkward positions. If you practice only in pleasant conditions, you will not be prepared for actual hunting situations. Practice during stormy weather, when you're tired, and from different positions and angles. Then you'll make tough hunting shots naturally, because, in practice, you've been there and done that.

### In the Field:

Just as your bow can change in storage, it can change or get knocked out of adjustment during the season, and only regular shooting throughout the fall will reveal problems. You also must shoot regularly to maintain your form, strength and shooting eye.

To practice during the season, take a target butt to camp for midday shooting. And carry a practice arrow — tipped with a rubber blunt or Judo head — in your quiver, so you can shoot in the field while hunting.

## JUMPING THE STRING

*Is an animal jumping the string a reality or an excuse for a poor shot? Answer — in a given situation it could be both. However, a deer can hear and jump the string. Make sure your bow is quiet. Sound travels at 1100 feet per second; the fastest arrow from a compound bow moves at 250 to 300 feet per second. String sound reaches the deer first, giving it a split second to react before the arrow arrives. A tense or nervous deer is more likely to react quickly than one that is feeding or resting. Oddly enough, when you are close, the louder noise is more likely to cause a violent reaction.*

*Quiet your bow by installing string silencers, keeping all bow screws tight, avoiding noisy quivers, silencing the arrow rest, installing a stabilizer. Arrow speed alone is not the answer to string jumping. A quiet bow and careful hunting techniques are the best ways to eliminate the old excuse, "He jumped the string!"*

*Portable stands allow you to change ambush sites quickly and quietly.*

# Quick & Easy Stands

### By Dwight Schuh

*For flexibility, you can't beat a portable.*

**B**ig, luxurious tree stands are okay for some purposes, but in many cases, small, light, quick stands are more practical. That's true if you have to travel far to hunt, as I often do, and scout and put up stands on the run, or if you hunt off-road and pack your stands long distances. And it's true if you want to stay flexible. Deer activity shifts regularly, and many hunters change stand locations daily to keep up with these trends.

In addition, leaving a stand in the woods just invites someone to steal it or to climb up and use it, leading to conflicts or fights. And, finally, in some places, it's illegal to leave stands in the woods. All these reasons make quick stands the ideal choice.

## Stands:

A quick stand is one that's light and portable, the kind you can pack around with you and put up on the spur of the moment. I like mine to weigh less than 10 pounds, preferably six to eight. The stand must be compact enough to fit in a daypack, or to serve *as* a daypack. It must be easy to put up. And it must be quick. You should be able to put up the stand and start hunting in 20 minutes maximum. With the right system and plenty of practice, some hunters can pick a tree and be ready to shoot in five minutes.

Choice of stand type depends on the kinds of trees available, your carrying method, personal preference and other variables. Even in identical circumstances, preferences differ. In Alabama, I hunted with two experienced hunters, one of whom used nothing but a sling-type stand, while the other insisted on a rope-on, platform stand.

CLIMBING STANDS — Where trees have straight trunks with few limbs, climbing stands seem natural. I like the security of the platform under my feet — as opposed to tree steps — while climbing. On the right tree, I can be in hunting position in less than 10 minutes. One morning while scouting in Idaho, I found some scrapes, ascended a tree with a climbing stand, and two hours later shot an 8-point buck.

With all climbing stands, you strap your feet to the platform, cock it away from the tree, pull it up, and then tip the platform horizontally to bite back into the tree.

That's pretty standard. But methods for pulling yourself up vary. With some stands, you sit on a seat and then alternately stand and sit to climb the tree. These may be the easiest to use, but many sit-stand climbers are heavy and bulky, not ideal quick stands. With lighter models, a light-weight seat doubles as a hand climber; you lean on the seat as you pull up the platform, raise the seat, lean on it, and so forth. To further reduce weight, you can leave the seat home and simply hug the tree to pull yourself up. Hug-climbing can be strenuous if you're not in shape, however.

Climbing aids such as Loc-On's Rope-N-Stick, a bar with a rope that twists around the tree, enable you to pull yourself up to ease strain on the arms and chest.

Climbers can be dangerous on wet, smooth-barked trees. One day I started to descend a wet aspen tree when my stand took off like a runaway elevator, and I found myself hanging by a safety belt. That's a thrill I didn't need. On wet trees, climbers may not be the best choice. (The need for a safety belt goes without saying.) Climbers can be a little noisy, especially as you bolt the climbing arm around a tree, and they're heavier, on average, than many fixed-position stands, although the total system may not weigh much, if any, more when you add steps to the fixed stand.

Amacker introduced a new climbing concept this year called the Hook, which consists of two small climbing stands, one strapped to each foot. In essence, you walk up the tree and then bind the individual stands in place to form a foot platform and seat. I haven't used the Hook in hunting, but in tests I found it fairly easy to use, even for climbing around limbs, which you can't do with standard climbers. The most obvious drawback is weight.

FIXED-POSITION STANDS — If wet bark, limbs or other obstacles prevent use of a climbing stand, a fixed-position stand is the obvious alternative. In fact, many hunters prefer fixed stands regardless of conditions, figuring they can put up such a stand almost as quickly, and more quietly, than they can a climber. Many manufacturers say they sell two to three times as many fixed-position stands as climbers. For a given platform size, fixed stands generally weigh less and pack easier because they have no climbing mechanism. Many fixed-position stands have a built-in seat, although some have a separate seat, and the lightest have no seat at all.

Attachment methods vary, but the most common are probably chain

## CHECK REGS

*Check your local regulations. Hunting laws in your area may make using portable stands your only sensible choice. Some states or areas have declared leaving stands in trees overnight illegal.*

and polypropylene rope. Some hunters prefer the chain because it's easy to use and can be locked to a tree, and it never deteriorates. The rope is equally easy, it's quieter, and is actually stronger. Comparing rope and chain, you instantly have suspicions about the rope, but the tensile strength exceeds that of most chains used on stands. A friend of mine didn't believe that, so he tied together the chain and rope from two tree stands, attached one end to his tractor, the other end to a tree, and started pulling. The chain broke. Rope will fray and weather, however, so it should be inspected regularly and replaced at the first signs of wear.

## SELF-CLIMBING STAND

Some stands attach to the tree with a strap and ratchet-tightening mechanism. And a fourth style hangs from a steel pin screwed into the tree with a backup strap around the tree for added safety. Pin-up stands are convenient, although the pin can be hard to screw into pines and other pitchy trees.

## SLING STAND

SLINGS — These consist of nylon webbing in which you hang from the tree in a sitting position. They're ideal for super-light hunting where you might pack in and take a one-evening stand over an elk wallow or mule deer trail. To get up the tree, you climb on limbs or tree steps, as with a fixed-position stand.

Slings restrict movement to some extent, preventing shots at certain angles, particularly behind you with a bow. With no foot support, they can bind your backside after long hours of sitting, so they may not be the best choice for prolonged hunting in one place. In trees with big limbs, you can often use a limb as a foot platform, or you can modify a sling by adding a rigid seat. Dr. Bob Sheppard, an Alabama whitetail fanatic, modified an Anderson Tree Sling by adding a padded plywood seat, and this is the only stand he uses during nearly 100 days of deer hunting each year.

## Climbing Methods:

TREE STEPS — With fixed-position and sling stands, screw-in steps are most popular, either one piece or folding. I've used both and don't see much difference in convenience or weight. Folding steps can rust or freeze, making them hard to open. The main thing to look for is sharp points that start easily. A climbing belt isn't essential because you can screw in the steps with one hand while holding on with the other, but a belt increases safety. Broken steps cause accidents. Always inspect your tree steps.

In some places you can't legally use screw-in steps, so strap-on or rope-on are the next choice. Some hunters prefer these anyway, because they're easier and faster if you're practiced at using them. A climbing belt *is* essential for these because you need both hands to strap each step to the tree. Installing strap-on steps without a belt is more than hard work; it's suicidal. API makes a good climbing belt with all-steel hardware that converts to a safety belt once you're in the stand. It has a built-in bow sling.

DRILL AND BOLTS — In place of steps, some hunters drill holes in the tree and drop bolts into the holes as steps. Southland Hunting Products makes a lightweight, folding drill called the Easy-Up Climbing System for boring holes. Southland recommends Grade 8, case-hardened cap screws for steps. This company also makes a good climbing belt, a necessity for placing bolts or tree steps (the plastic buckle concerns me a little). In place of a hand drill, some hunters carry a cordless electric drill.

CLIMBING SPIKES – Sport Climbers strap around the ankles with spikes that jab into the tree. Used with a climbing belt, they're fast and convenient. But they require practice and caution. Bob Sheppard tells about a hunter who'd climbed 15 feet up a tree with spikes and was sawing off a limb when he noticed a big hornet's nest on the limb. Too late! The limb, sawed nearly through, swung down and slammed into the tree. As hornets boiled out, the hunter, making a hasty exit, missed a step and gashed his leg with a spike. Sheppard wasn't sure whether the spike or the hornets did more damage.

CLIMBING STICKS – These consist of a long rod made of three- to four-foot sections with built-in steps. They may be the fastest climbing method of all and one of the safest, but climbing sticks are bulkier and heavier than climbing steps. You wouldn't pack them into the back-country, but for quick hunts near access points, they're great.

## Accessories:

Lightweight pruning shears and a small folding saw are needed to clear shooting lanes and remove limbs for climbing. A bow stand or screw-in hanger gives you a place to stand a bow, hang a rifle, or store other gear. An auxiliary seat like the Lewis & Lewis Bun Buddy adds comfort to a stand that consists only of a platform, or you can use a sling stand as seat/safety belt. Add a tow rope for hauling bow or rifle into the stand, a safety belt or climbing harness for safety, and a light pack for carrying accessories, and you're ready for quick stand hunting anywhere.

## Safety:

Falls from trees account for a high percentage of hunting accidents. It's important to understand that all tree stand accidents are self-inflicted; a fall victim can blame no one but himself.

Equipment failure, particularly broken steps, accounts for some accidents. Constantly inspect gear for weak points. The most dangerous moments come as you're hanging from or climbing into a stand, or trimming limbs. To free your hands for securing a stand, hang the stand on a step screwed into the tree. And never climb up into a stand. Instead, place your steps at least as high as, or higher than, the stand and step down onto the platform.

Always wear a safety belt as you climb and prepare your stand. Several companies make climbing belts that double as safety belts once you're on stand. A climbing belt not only protects you from falling as you climb – with both climbing stands and steps – but also relieves strain as you install steps, hang stands, and trim limbs. Amacker makes one with two loops for use with the Hook. As you go around limbs, you attach a loop above the limb before releasing the one below so you're always protected against falling.

The need for safety belts has been so belabored that it hardly seems worth repeating. But some people won't learn. You wear a safety belt not just to catch you if you fall, but also to prevent your falling. Some belts have no adjusters, just loops at each end, which leaves two to three feet of slack between you and the tree. Bad scene. Use an adjustable belt that eliminates slack.

### STRAP-ON STAND

*Hunter using screw-in steps (below).*

### TREE STEPS

# Building a Permanent Stand

*By Jay Cassell*

*If you have access to the perfect spot, this project may be for you.*

If you intend to build your own permanent tree stand, first make sure that it's okay in your hunting area. In my case, the land is owned privately, and the owner gave me the go-ahead. If you hunt on state land, you'll have to go with a portable, as it's illegal to build there.

However, if you are in a situation where you can build a permanent stand, the next thing to do is scout the area thoroughly. Once you've found the spot, the planning begins. In my case, I found a sturdy, forked beech tree that overlooked the exact area I wanted to watch. Next, I made a sketch of my proposed stand, and then gathered the necessary materials. With the help of two friends (one of whom had an ATV for transport), we set to it.

First we cut down a third, nearby beech, about the same diameter as the forked tree. We topped it so that its total height was about 20 feet, then carried it over to the forked beech and pushed it upright so that it leaned against it. With a flat rock for a support under our makeshift corner post, we chain-sawed some of the 2x4s in half. These we nailed into the corner post and then into both living trees, as supports, to form a triangle with the trees.

Moving up the trees, we constructed another level of support, then started on the floor. Here, again, we nailed two halves of a 2x4 onto the corner post and real trees, to form another triangle. We then cut the 1x6s into three-foot and two-foot sections, which we nailed on top of the 2x4s for floorboards. A railing went on next, about three feet above the floor; then, three feet above that, we put on the roof, using the same method we used for the floor. Some shingles on the roof, some trimming of excess woodland overhangs, and the basic structure was complete. There was even enough wood left over to fashion a seat, with two short lengths of 2x4s nailed between the back two trees, and a few pieces of 1x6s nailed on top! Spikes were nailed into the side of one of the live trees to serve as the ladder. Next year, I may even add plywood or camouflage-netting sides to block the wind and further conceal myself.

A few thoughts here. We found it necessary to cut down the third tree, as I didn't want to change the location of my stand and there was no third tree close enough to incorporate into the stand. If you can find three (or four) trees growing close together, or one sturdy tree that splits into three trees as it goes up – "triangle trees," I call them – by all means use them. Live trees will be sturdier, and last longer, than dead ones or a combination of live and dead ones. A large double tree, for that matter, can also become an excellent tree stand.

On the subject of picking a tree, make certain that your tree is in good shape before you start building on it. The last thing you want to do is build a tree stand in a set of trees that may rot out in a few years.

When building a stand, do it in spring or summer. Deer know the forest, and anything out of the ordinary is going to be suspect to them. If you build your stand well before hunting season, they'll get used to seeing it there, and won't view it as potentially dangerous. Building it during summer will also give the wood some time to weather, so it won't stand out once the leaves have fallen.

If you somehow find yourself in a situation where you must build a tree stand just before or during hunting season, it might make sense to use natural wood, as the deer may not notice it as readily. I generally prefer 2x4s from the lumberyard, however, as they last longer, and are easier to work with. Natural wood is wet, too, which means it's more apt to split.

Once your stand is completed, go sit in it for a while. Like the

view? If not, it might pay to carry a limb pruner or handsaw into the woods and clear shooting lanes and any limbs that obscure your vision.

Finally, clean up the ground around your stand. Let the woods revert to its natural state; the less human odor and evidence of human presence, the better. Never urinate near your stand, before or during deer season, as you'll simply be advertising your presence to the deer. For that matter, you should use scent on your boots, to further mask your presence.

*A bit of work in the summer will pay off come autumn (below).*

# The *Height* of *Foolishness*

By Thomas McIntyre

*Life's too short; no deer is worth a tumble from a tree.*

*Regardless of your tree stand's height, you should always wear a safety strap.*

**A** friend used to give me the willies every deer hunting season by lashing on a pair of climbing spikes, slinging his portable onto his back, then monkeying 30 feet up a tree in the dark to where he'd somehow tie on his stand, climb into it, pull his muzzleloader up after him and proceed to fall soundly asleep!

How this guy managed to survive remains one of life's unfathomable mysteries. Obviously, good sense had no hand in it, because hunters, even the most experienced, fall from tree stands; many are injured, and some die.

According to the International Hunter Education Organization's 1995 *Hunting Accident Report,* 13 hunters died last year nationwide as the result of "self-inflicted" tree stand accidents, nearly double the 1994 figure of seven. Statistics on nonfatal tree stand accidents are difficult to gather, as only those requiring hospitalization are recorded. A recent survey by the National Bowhunter Education Foundation did report, however, that 63 percent of the hunters polled admitted to falling out of their tree stands at one time or another during their hunting careers, half of such accidents occurring while they were climbing. More than 83 percent of these "victims" were not wearing a fall restraint; fewer than 49 percent reported always wearing one.

## Meeting the Standards:

In the National Bowhunter Education Foundation survey cited above, 23 percent of tree stand accidents were attributed to "structural failure," which usually means an old 2x4 nailed between two dead limbs finally rotting through. Tree stand manufacturers, though, faced with what in insurance parlance is referred to as a severe "exposure" problem, decided a couple of years ago to join together to establish safety standards for the industry, including warning labels and improved hands-on instruction in safe tree stand use. Some 30 manufacturers (among them Warren and Sweat, Summit, Loc-On and Trophy Whitetail) will submit their products for independent testing of impact resistance, load capacity, stability, tree adherence and repetitive use — that last test equal to a hunter's climbing in and out of his tree stand twice a day for a 60-day season for 20 years. If they pass, the products will receive an Archery Manufacturers and Merchants Organization seal of approval. Look for such seals on hang-on stands this fall or next spring. Similar standards are being developed for ladder, tripod and climbing stands, steps and fall restraints.

## TO HUNT SAFELY ABOVE THE GROUND, FOLLOW THESE SIMPLE RULES

**The object of hunting from an elevated stand is to make it easier for us to spot game, and more difficult for game to detect us, not for us to experience sudden impact with the earth or to end up looking like the Hanged Man in the tarot. To minimize the risks of tree stand hunting, there are a number of basic precautions to take:**

- *Make certain that a friend or family member knows exactly where you will be hunting before you go afield.*

- *Practice putting up your tree stand while standing on steps only a foot or two off the ground.*

- *Never wear your stand (or any other piece of equipment) while climbing; it only gives you something worse than the ground to land on.*

- *Tie your haul line to your belt, not your stand, for easy access.*

- *When at your tree, place your equipment on the ground opposite the side that you are climbing; should you fall, you'll avoid landing on it.*

- *Secure your stand to larger trees for greater contact.*

- *Use chain- or strap-on steps. They are generally more reliable than screw-in models.*

- *Check all nuts and bolts on the tree stand before climbing in it.*

- *Avoid heights much above 15 or 20 feet, since they do not significantly increase hunting success. In some cases, going higher may decrease your chances.*

- *Always wear a safety belt or, better, a harness. Examine all buckles, D-rings and hooks to make sure everything is sound; and wear your harness or belt neither too low, to avoid dangling upside down in the event of a fall, nor too high, to prevent asphyxiation.*

- *Never haul a loaded weapon in or out of a tree stand.*

- *Be in good enough condition to climb easily.*

- *Keep your survival gear (knife, matches, compass, whistle) on you, not hanging from a limb in your daypack, in case you do fall. If you do make an unplanned exit from your stand, evaluate your condition before moving.*

# Recognize These Guys?

*By Peter J. Fiduccia*

*Finally, the arrival of effective decoys.*

**U**sing decoys to hunt whitetails is relatively new, but the hunting technique itself can be traced back to the Native Americans. These efficient hunters understood the whitetail's curious nature, and covered themselves with hides (including the head and, sometimes, antlers) to attract and stalk closer to the deer. Today's sportsmen can take advantage of the whitetail's inquisitiveness by using a variety of decoys and decoying tactics. Many models are available. Some are portable, some semi-permanent; all can add an effective dimension to your hunting.

## Mounted Doe Heads:

About 20 years ago, during archery season, I thought about using a decoy to lure in deer that traditionally hung up 50 to 60 yards from my stand when I called to them. At the time, there weren't any high-tech, lightweight decoys on the market, so I nailed a mounted doe head onto a tree, and hung a stuffed deer rump on the opposite side. (I used this tactic only on private property.) The decoy worked! However, taking it into and out of the woods was a chore, not to mention risky. Consequently, I began using a real deer tail. It was easy to carry and set up, and safe to use.

## The Tale of the Tail:

Since then, when I take a deer I always keep the tail, cleaning it and combing it free of debris, then spreading it out to dry. Tails can be kept in the freezer during the off-season. Every September, I take out a tail or two, cut a small hole in the hide at the base of each (large enough to pass a string through), and hang them outside to air out and soften up.

Whether you call or stand hunt, a deer tail decoy can make the difference between seeing and not seeing deer. In states where this decoy is legal, hang the tail 10 to 20 yards from your stand in semi-open cover at the height of a mature deer's rump (28 to 32 inches). Sprinkle scent (doe-in-estrus or tarsal) onto the tail, then attach at least 30 yards of string to it. If you are hunting from the ground, tie the string around your forearm. If you are hunting from a tree stand, tie it around your ankle. Gently tug the string several times every half hour — just enough to make it move from side to side. I often make a blat call while doing this. Passing deer spot the movement, hear the call, and move closer to investigate.

Deer can spot a twitching tail from great distances. I have used this tactic many times to bring in deer that are more than 100 yards away from my stand.

## Full-Size Decoys:

Over the past few years, I have videotaped deer reactions to different full-size decoys set up in various positions. Full-size decoys are especially attractive to deer because of their realistic shape and appearance. Other animals find them convincing, too.

Two years ago, a black bear boar entered my food plot, spotted a life-size "small buck feeding" decoy (which was facing away from him), and proceeded to stalk and attack it. He pounced on the back of the decoy and when it collapsed to the ground, bit its neck and removed a large chunk of plastic foam in a single bite. He continued to rip large chunks from it, and within a few minutes had totally dismembered the decoy. Then he left – but not without carrying off the hindquarters.

One reason the bear was not spooked by the decoy is that he didn't detect any human odors on it. When setting up any type of decoy – mounted, natural, cloth or full-size synthetic – never touch it with bare hands; use rubber gloves. If you can't do this, spray the decoy with a scent block before applying a natural scent to it.

When you are shopping for life-size decoys, look for ones that are light-weight, easy to put together and come with anchors. Decoys that cannot be secured will be problematic – especially when deer get coy and begin to smell, nudge or try to mount them.

## Setup Strategies:

Don't just walk into the woods and set up a decoy. Using a decoy properly requires planning and coordination. Once you have assembled your decoy, set it up in an area offering good cover and a clean shot. This is crucial, because deer will often come in to a decoy quickly and leave just as fast. If you're using a buck decoy, don't be surprised if a real buck comes charging out of cover, knocks over the decoy and bounds off. In such situations, having a clear shooting lane is crucial.

## Other Tactics:

Life-size decoys are available in different positions, in doe and buck models. I have had most success when using a doe decoy in the "ready" position. On occasion, this visual stimulation alone has been enough to prompt bucks to run to the decoy instead of walk. I have also had success with buck decoys during the rut; they often generate responses from larger, aggressive bucks that want to chase away the challenger.

Try to place the decoy with its head facing away from the direction of the deer's probable approach. Deer that are hesitant about approaching a decoy concentrate on the face. When they can't see the face, they zero in on the decoy itself, thereby giving a hunter more time to take steady aim.

Other wildlife decoys can be used to attract or calm whitetails. I'll often place a turkey or crow decoy about 30 yards in front of the deer decoy. Approaching deer perceive it to be looking at the bird decoy, and are reassured. On the other end of the scale, I have placed scarecrow-type decoys in tree stands as early as July to get deer accustomed to the presence of a human figure. I have also used the human decoy during hunting season to move deer off their trails and into an area where I am posted.

Always keep safety and legality in mind when using decoys. Even on private land, be especially careful. Like the bear in my yard, another hunter could also be fooled by a well-placed decoy.

# Field-Dressing Whitetails

*Proper care of wild game in the field assures that the meat you bring home will be in prime condition for the table.*

Follow the step-by-step instructions on these pages to field-dress your deer. Immediate dressing drains off blood and dissipates body heat. Wear rubber gloves to protect you from any parasites or blood-borne diseases the animal may be carrying, and to make cleanup easier.

Follow state regulations requiring evidence of the sex on the carcass. Where the law allows, attach the registration tag after field-dressing, rather than before. It may get torn off during the dressing procedure.

*– Editors at Creative Publishing international*

**1.** Locate the base of the breastbone by pressing on the center of the ribcage until you feel its end. Make a shallow cut that is long enough to insert the first two fingers of your left hand. Be careful not to puncture the intestines when cutting.

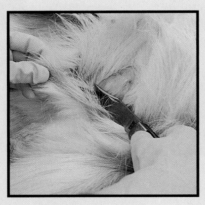

**2.** Form a V with the first two fingers of your left hand. Hold the knife between your fingers with the cutting edge up, as shown. Cut through the abdominal wall to the pelvic area. Your fingers prevent you from puncturing the intestines.

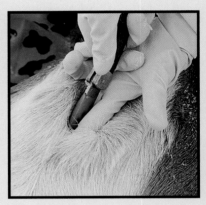

**3.** Separate the external reproductive organs of a buck from the abdominal wall, but do not cut them off completely. Remove the udder of a doe if it was still nursing. The milk sours rapidly, and could give the meat an unpleasant flavor.

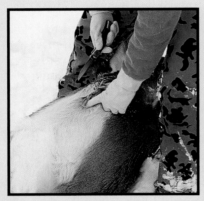

**4.** Straddle the animal, facing its head. Unless you plan to mount the head, cut the skin from the base of the breastbone to the jaw, with the cutting edge of the knife up. If you plan to mount the head, follow your taxidermist's instructions.

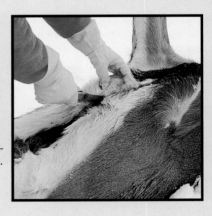

**5.** Brace your elbows against your legs, with your left hand supporting your right. Cut through the center of the breastbone, using your knees to provide leverage. If the animal is old or very large, you may need to use a game saw or small axe.

**6.** Slice between the hams to free a buck's urethra, or if you elect to split the pelvic bone on either a buck or doe. Make careful cuts around the urethra until it is freed to a point just above the anus. Be careful not to sever the urethra.

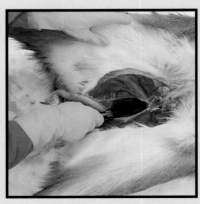

**7.** Cut around the anus; on a doe, the cut should also include the reproductive opening (above the anus). Free the rectum and urethra by loosening the connective tissue with your knife. Tie off the rectum and urethra with kitchen string (inset).

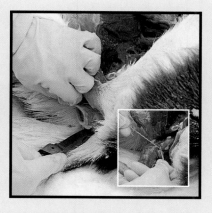

**8.** Free the windpipe and esophagus by cutting the connective tissue. Sever windpipe and esophagus at the jaw. Grasp them firmly and pull down, continuing to cut where necessary, until freed to the point where the windpipe branches out into the lungs.

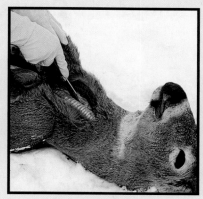

**9.** Hold ribcage open on one side with left hand. Cut the diaphragm, from the rib opening down to the backbone. Stay as close to the ribcage as possible; do not puncture the stomach. Repeat on other side so the cuts meet over the backbone.

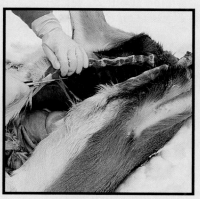

**10.** Remove the heart by severing the connecting blood vessels. Hold the heart upside down for a few moments to drain excess blood. Place heart in a plastic bag. Some hunters find it easier to remove the entrails first, then take the heart and liver from the gutpile.

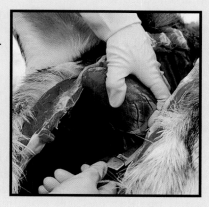

**11.** Cut the tubes that attach the liver, and remove it. Check liver for spots, cysts or scarring, which could indicate parasites or disease. If you see any, discard the liver. If liver is clean, place into plastic bag with heart. Place on ice as soon as possible.

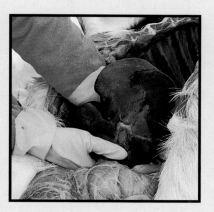

**12.** Pull tied-off rectum and urethra underneath the pelvic bone and into the body cavity, unless you have split the pelvic bone. (If you have, this is unnecessary.) Roll the animal on its side so the entrails begin to spill out the side of the body cavity.

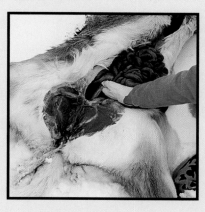

**13.** Grasp the windpipe and esophagus firmly. Pull down and away from the animal's body. If the organs do not pull away freely, the diaphragm may still be partially attached. Scoop from both ends toward the middle to finish rolling out the entrails.

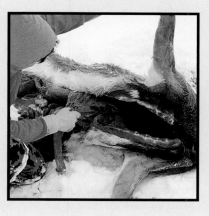

**14.** Sponge cavity clean, and prop open with a stick. If the urinary tract or intestines have been severed, wash meat with snow or clean water. If you must leave the animal, drape it over brush or logs with the cavity down, or hang it from a tree to speed cooling.

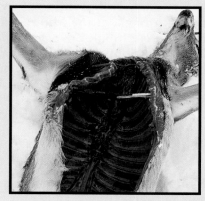

# ABOUT THE CONTRIBUTORS

## Gerald Almy

Gerald Almy lives with his wife and daughter in a log home in the foothills of Little North Mountain in the Shenandoah Valley of Virginia. He has hunted whitetails in over half of the states, as well as Mexico and Canada, for nearly 30 years. Since graduating Phi Beta Kappa from the State University of New York at Binghamton with a degree in English, he has pursued a full-time career as an outdoor writer, authoring two books and several thousand magazine and newspaper articles. He has won numerous awards for his writing and today is Field Editor for *Sports Afield*.

## Scott Bestul

Scott Bestul sold his first story, a deer hunting article, to *Sports Afield* in 1988. He has written extensively on whitetail hunting tactics for a variety of national magazines. Scott and his wife, Shari, live in rural southeastern Minnesota, in the heart of some of the Midwest's finest deer hunting country. Scott currently serves as Regional Editor for *Field & Stream*.

## Mike Bleech

Mike Bleech is a full-time freelance outdoor writer/photographer. The pursuit of deer has taken him from the Gulf of St. Lawrence to the Gulf of Mexico and westward to the Rocky Mountains. He has hunted deer with slugs for over 30 years.

## Philip Bourjaily

Philip Bourjaily lives in Iowa City, Iowa, and hunts throughout the Midwest. He's been a frequent contributor to *Sports Afield* and today he is Contributing Editor to *Field & Stream*. He is coauthor (with his father, novelist Vance Bourjaily) of the book *Fishing by Mail* (1993) and is also Ducks Unlimited's 1997 Wetlands Conservation Achievement Award Winner.

## Monte Burch

Monte Burch has been hunting deer with bow, gun and camera since killing his first whitetail with a homemade Osage orange bow while still in his teens. He's hunted deer over much of North America and has been writing about deer hunting for over 30 years for almost all the major hunting magazines. Monte is currently Contributing Editor for *Sports Afield* and has authored three books on deer hunting.

## Jay Cassell

Jay Cassell caught his first fish when he was 6 years old — a bluefish, from Long Island Sound — and shot his first whitetail in the Allagash region of Maine about 20 years later. He has hunted across North America, from caribou in Alaska and elk in Wyoming, to whitetails in Canada, Texas, Alabama, Mississippi, Wyoming, Delaware, Maine and his home state of New York. His numerous hunting and fishing articles have been published in *Outdoor Life* and in many other publications. He is the editor of *The Best of Sports Afield*, a book published in August 1996 by Grove Atlantic. Today, Jay is Contributing Editor for *Outdoor Life*.

## Peter J. Fiduccia

Peter J. Fiduccia, Editor in Chief of the Outdoorsman's Edge Book Club, is an award-winning author and producer. His deer-hunting techniques are shared with readers through regular deer-hunting features in magazines, newspaper columns, radio shows, books he has authored and his television series. He has also been the featured speaker at numerous outdoor show deer seminars. Peter is a member of OWAA and many other outdoor organizations in his home state of New York. Peter's book, *Whitetail Strategies — A No-Nonsense Approach to Successful Deer Hunting*, magazine features and seminars mark him as one of the true deer-hunting experts in America today.

## Grits Gresham

Grits Gresham has written for more than three decades and today serves as Shooting Editor for *Guns & Ammo*. He has hunted throughout America, six countries in Africa, and in Europe, South America, Mexico and Canada. His features on game management and conservation reflect his graduate degree in wildlife management and his years of game and fish work on federal, state and private levels. He has appeared on network television for more than 30 years as host/commentator for series covering shooting, hunting and fishing and is currently host of the "Shooting Sports America" TV series on ESPN.

## Tom Gresham

An award-winning photographer (1996 Shooting Sports Writer of the Year), Tom hosts "Tom Gresham's Gun Talk", his own nationally syndicated radio show and cohosts "Chevy Trucks Shooting Sports America", a television series. Having served as an editor for several magazines, Tom is Founder and Publisher of Cane River Publishing. He has also written three books and coauthored another. Tom also does consulting on firearms issues.

## Tom McIntyre

Tom McIntyre's hunting has taken him to five (and soon, six) continents, but he always manages to come home for deer. Field Editor of *Sports Afield* magazine, he is author of three books about hunting and fishing: *Days Afield, The Way of the Hunter,* and his latest, *Dreaming the Lion* (published by Countrysport). Tom has also written for the *Los Angeles Times, Gray's Sporting Journal,* and *The Field* in England. In 1997 he profiled General H. Norman Schwarzkopf for *The Shooting Field,* a quarterly published by the gunmakers Holland and Holland. Aside from his award-winning journalism, he is at work on a fantasy-adventure novel for children and holds a second-degree black belt in Aikido. He, his wife, Elaine, and their young son, Bryan Ruark, live in Wyoming.

## Don Oster

Executive Editor of Creative Publishing international's Outdoor Group, Don Oster has been an avid hunter since age 10. He cut his teeth on small game in Southern Indiana, where he grew up, subsequently graduating to big game. Don hunts with bow, rifle and muzzleloader. A former bass tournament angler, he wrote *Largemouth Bass* in the Freshwater Angler Series™.

## Aaron Fraser Pass

Aaron Fraser Pass is a freelance writer and photographer specializing in sporting, wildlife conservation and technical firearms topics. Over the past 25 years, Pass has covered everything from shooting driven grouse in Scotland to hunting whitetail deer and wild turkey literally in his backyard in the foothills of the southern Appalachian Mountains of north Georgia. He has served in editorial capacities with several regional and national sporting magazines and currently is a Field Editor to *Sports Afield*.

## Clair Rees

A full-time writer and firearms authority, Clair Rees has been a frequent *Sports Afield* contributor. His work has also appeared in more than 70 national magazines, including *Field & Stream, Guns, Guns & Ammo* and *Reader's Digest*. The author of ten books on hunting, firearms, backpacking and off-road driving, Clair has twice received Anschutz's "Outdoor Writer of the Year" award.

## Dwight Schuh

Bowhunting since about 1970, Dwight Schuh has taken 15 species of North American big game. He especially likes planning his own backcountry hunts for deer, elk and other wilderness species. Living in Idaho with his wife, Laura, and two daughters, Dwight serves as Editor for *Bowhunter* magazine and as Field Editor for *Sports Afield*.

## Wayne van Zwoll

Wayne van Zwoll has published three books and more than 300 magazine articles on hunting and shooting. A big-game guide and competitive rifleman, Wayne also writes and lectures on optics. He teaches marksmanship at outdoor schools for women.

Contributors (Note: T=Top, C=Center, B=Bottom, L=Left, R=Right, I=Inset)

PHOTOGRAPHERS:

**Charles J. Alsheimer**
Bath, New York
© *Charles J. Alsheimer: back cover C; pp. 15, 17, 18B, 20, 26-27, 38, 42, 66, 70, 80-81, 108*

**Scott Bestul**
Lewiston, Minnesota
© *Scott Bestul: p. 14*

**Denver Bryan**
DenverBryan.com
© *Denver Bryan: p. 85B*

**Amos Chan**
New York, New York
© *Amos Chan: pp. 104-105, 106-107*

**Robert DiScalfani**
New York, New York
© *Robert DiScalfani: pp. 122-123*

**Donald M. Jones**
Troy, Montana
© *Donald M. Jones: pp. 11, 16, 19, 46, 50, 58, 84BL, 119*

**Mark Kayser**
Pierre, South Dakota
© *Mark Kayser: front cover, back cover TL*

**Bill Kinney**
BillKinney.com
© *Bill Kinney: back cover T; pp. 6-7, 18T, 21, 28, 36, 52, 54-55, 72, 83, 84TL*

**Lance Krueger**
McAllen, Texas
© *Lance Krueger: pp. 4, 8, 35, 43, 53, 56, 60, 65, 85T, 90-91, 114, 117T, 120*

**Bill Lea**
Franklin, North Carolina
© *Bill Lea: pp. 9, 25, 84R*

**Stephen W. Maas**
Wyoming, Minnesota
© *Stephen W. Maas: pp. 10, 117B*

**Bill Marchel**
BillMarchel.com
© *Bill Marchel: pp. 32-33*

**Aaron Fraser Pass**
Buford, Georgia
© *Aaron Fraser Pass: p. 102 all*

ILLUSTRATORS:

**William Bramhall**
Riley Illustration
New York, New York
© *William Bramhall: pp. 76-79 all*

**Gary Cooley**
Franklin, Michigan
© *Gary Cooley: pp. 22-23*

**Gary Gretter**
Sandy Hook, Conneticut
© *Gary Gretter: pp. 39-41 all*

MANUFACTURERS:

**Anderson Tree Sling**
Saddle Brook, New Jersey
*Sling stand on page 116B*

**Lowrance Electronics**
12000 E. Skelly Drive
Tulsa, Oklahoma 74128
*GPS unit on page 31TL*

*Acknowledgment is given for the following:*

• "Deer Hunting's Terrible 10" copyright © 1994, "The Muzzleloading Revolution" and "Snow Bucks" copyright © 1996 used by permission of Gerald Almy

• "Whitetails & Acorns" copyright © 1993 used by permission of Scott Bestul

• "Slug-Gunning for Deer" copyright © 1995 used by permission of Mike Bleech & Philip Bourjaily

• "The Magnificent Seven" copyright © 1996 and "Tips for Opening Day" copyright © 1997 used by permission of Monte Burch

• "Find Your Buck Now" copyright © 1996 used by permission of Monte Burch and Peter J. Fiduccia

• "Building a Permanent Stand" copyright © 1993 "Late Season Is Drive Time" copyright © 1996, "The Still-Hunting Advantage" copyright © 1996, "Talk to the Animals" copyright © 1997 used by permission of Jay Cassell

• "Deer Sign Language" copyright © 1992, "Secrets of the Rut" copyright © 1993, "Recognize These Guys" and "Whitetail Tactics for Three Stages of the Rut" copyright © 1995, "Deer Tricks" copyright 1996 used by permission of Peter J. Fiduccia

• "Handgunning for Deer" copyright © 1993, "The Point of Aim" copyright © 1995 used by permission of Tom Gresham

• "The Quest for Accuracy" copyright © 1993 used by permission of Grits Gresham

• "The Height of Foolishness" copyright © 1996 used by permission of Tom McIntyre

• "The Troubled Shooter" copyright © 1996 used by permission of Aaron Fraser Pass

• "Easy Shooting Rifles" copyright © 1993 used by permission of Clair Rees

• "Quick & Easy Stands" copyright © 1992, "The Human Scent Factor" copyright © 1993, "Patterning Whitetails" copyright © 1994, "How Whitetails Move" copyright © 1995, and "Get That Bow Out of the Closet" copyright © 1997 used by permission of Dwight Schuh

• "How Scopes Help You Hit" copyright © 1993 used by permission of Wayne van Zwoll